REBUILDING GOD'S PEOPLE

Rebuilding God's People

Strategies for Revitalizing Declining Churches

Michael McCutcheon

CHRISTIAN PUBLICATIONS
Camp Hill, Pennsylvania

Christian Publications
3825 Hartzdale Drive, Camp Hill, PA 17011

The mark of ✝ vibrant faith

ISBN: 0-87509-505-4
LOC Catalog Card Number: 92-74654
© 1993 Christian Publications
All rights reserved
Printed in the United States of America

93 94 95 96 97   5   4   3   2   1

Table of Contents

Introduction

How This Got Started

I trusted Jesus Christ as my Lord and Savior while I was enlisted in the United States Air Force. Later, while I was still serving with the Air Force in Vietnam, I received my call to the ministry. Upon my discharge from military service, I went directly to Bible college. As a student there, I preached in the local county jail and later became director of an inner-city teen center in Columbia, South Carolina. Upon graduation from Bible college, I took a declining church for my first pastorate. Soon after that, I realized I had no idea at all what a pastor was to do or be—all my experience had been in parachurch ministries.

My lack of church experience prior to entering the pastorate was coupled with a desire to have a biblical model to follow. About the time of my second pastorate I began to see how the book of Nehemiah fulfilled the role of a biblical model for the ministry to which the Lord had called me—declining churches. Nehemiah also had accepted a call from the Lord to go to a discouraged, declining group of God's people. He was able to do what I wanted to do in my own ministry—he motivated the people, established and maintained a standard of excellence, reestablished God's testimony among them, developed lay leadership to carry on the work of the ministry and handled the criticism and opposition that "goes with the territory."

I believe that the book of Nehemiah is God's manual on leadership. As we study the life of Nehemiah, we will see some of the principles of leadership which God has placed in His Word. And these principles are just as valid today as in the days of Nehemiah. Declining churches can have new life and become dynamic, growing churches once again. That's the message of hope this book offers to any pastor of a declining church today.

Chapter 1

The Difference a Leader Makes

One simple definition of a leader is someone people are following. If a leader does not have someone following him, he is not leading; he is merely walking.

The record of Nehemiah's leadership in bringing the Israelites back to Jerusalem and rebuilding God's testimony among them has become very valuable to me as a pastor. In the book of Nehemiah, it is impossible to separate the man from his ministry; both are part of the same message. How Nehemiah set out to rebuild both the wall at Jerusalem and the testimony of God's people gives us an understanding of how to go about this same process of rebuilding a declining church. And as Nehemiah faced difficulties, handled his life priorities, and maintained a close walk with God, we see the development of the character of a man who sought to make a permanent difference in his world for the Lord.

In our study of leadership principles as demonstrated in the book of Nehemiah, three terms need to be defined: a declining ministry, a redevelopment pastor and growth in a ministry.

Why Churches Decline

A *declining ministry* is any gospel ministry that at one point flourished, but now is failing spiritually, physically and numerically, and is about to be dissolved. Though speaking here primarily of churches, it can apply to any Christian ministry.

Fictitious Faith Fellowship has joined the ranks of a declining ministry. It had once been a living, growing church with a dynamic ministry in the community. But lately its numbers have decreased and its ministry impact has been greatly reduced. Not many people attend the services—just the faithful few—and they are holding on for dear life. Finances are tight, bills do not get paid on time and the pastor has had to take a part-time job to make ends meet for his family. The church knows the next step is to close its doors and bring the ministry of FF to a close.

Everyone can think of an example of a declining church. Perhaps you pastor one. According to the *Winn Arn Church Growth Report*, Issue #21, 80 to 85 percent of the churches in the United States today are either plateaued or declining.[1] Coupled with that figure is the fact that the median church in the United States today averages 75 people in its Sunday morning service.[2] The average church today does not have to decline very long before it is in serious trouble.

Five Characteristics of Declining Churches

How do churches that were once alive and active become declining churches? Though there could be numerous reasons, I have observed five characteristics of declining ministries.

1. Trust in Success

When those in a successful ministry become spiritually satisfied and trust in the success of the ministry instead of the One who brought them success, the ministry will begin to decline. In Deuteronomy 8:11–17, God warned His people about a dangerous tendency that could set in after they conquered the promised land and were living comfortably there: to forget that God had accomplished all they enjoyed and to say that they themselves had brought it all about. Often success is wrongly attributed to the programs of the church rather than to the Person of Christ. When the Lord Jesus Christ is not the Head of the ministry and trust is placed in the programs and methods, sooner or later the church will decline.

2. Controlling Leadership

When the leadership of the church quits giving spiritual direction and begins controlling the ministry, it will decline. The apostle John wrote of such a person in Third John 9–10. Diotrephes was one who "loves to be first." Those placed in leadership need to be open to the guidance of the Holy Spirit and resist the tendency to take charge. If they forget and begin to exercise control over the ministry, sooner or later it will also decline.

The Lord would rather His work be stopped than to see it continue without regard to dependence upon Him and His Word. David learned this important lesson in Second Samuel 6:1–11 when he wanted to transport the ark of the covenant back to Jerusalem. A new cart was brought to transport the ark back to Jerusalem and a joyous procession went before to proclaim a celebration. All went well until the procession came to Nacon's threshing floor. Uzzah put out his hand to steady the ark on the cart and God struck him dead. David became angry at the Lord and refused to go any further. He gave the ark to Obed-Edom, a Gittite, and went back to Jerusalem.

Three months later David remembered that the way in which God had ordained that the ark be carried was not upon a new cart, but by the Levites according to the Word of God in Numbers 4:1ff. Putting something or someone upon a new cart was man's contemporary method of showing honor, but it was not the way the Lord God had said to move the ark. God would rather not have the ark come back to Jerusalem than have it carried using man's methods. I believe it is the same with churches. The Lord Jesus would rather a church decline and ultimately die than have it continue under an attitude of neglect or apathy toward His Word.

3. Lack of Balance

When a balance is not maintained between outreach (reaching the lost with the gospel) and maintenance (building up of those who are already saved and part of the local church), the ministry will decline. Normally, a good balance is when one third of personnel and resources are given to outreach functions and two thirds are given toward maintenance functions. When maintenance becomes the primary focus and outreach is non-existent, the church is on its way to becoming a declining ministry.

4. Centering on Leaders

When a ministry is "leadership-centered," it is a prime candidate to become a declining ministry. As Ephesians 4:11–12 tells us, God gives spiritual leaders in order to perfect, or equip, other Christians so that they in turn can do the work of the ministry and edify the body of Christ as a whole. But if the pastoral leadership does not train and equip lay leadership for ministry, that ministry will become leadership-centered (or leader-dependent) instead of people-centered.

Leader-dependent ministries are not good for either the people or the leader. In Exodus 18:13–27, Moses was involved in a leader-dependent ministry. When Jethro, Moses' father-in-law, saw what was going on he wisely told Moses it was not good for either him or his people. Jethro went on to give some positive direction as to how Moses could involve the spiritual men in the ministry of governing God's people with him. The results were that the people became involved and Moses' ministry was spared.

Leader-dependent ministries produce two negative results. Such ministries cause frustration among the people because they are not able to exercise the spiritual gifts that the Lord has given them. They feel a lack of purpose in the ministry and soon withdraw. And leader-dependent ministries can also cause burnout among the leadership because they have assumed more responsibility than the Lord intended them to have. They become overburdened, discouraged and soon give up or move on to another ministry.

5. Focusing on the Past

When people view the past as their "high-water mark," they lose vision for the future and become a declining ministry. As my friend Irving Malm has often reminded me, "God's purposes are always onward and upward and never downward or backward." In Ephesians 3:20–21, Scripture tells us that God is able to do beyond anything we can even comprehend if we let Him work in us and through us in order to give the Lord Jesus glory in His church. The moment we stop letting Him work in us and through us, the Lord Jesus will not receive present glory in His church and we will be forced to look backward to see evidences of the Lord's glory. In a ministry undertaken for the glory of the Lord Jesus Christ, we must anticipate the future with a mindset that says the best days are yet before us. Otherwise, the ministry will decay through a lack of vision and become a declining ministry.

Needed: Someone to Turn It Around

A second term that needs to be defined is *redevelopment pastor*. This is a pastor who has the heart of a learner and will accept a call of God to go to a declining ministry; he has the necessary knowledge and skills to halt the decline and bring about growth in the ministry for God's glory.

The local church has a twofold nature—it is both an organization and an organism. The church as an organization must have structure which allows it to grow. This organizational structure has two main aspects:

1. Make-up and procedures for decision making. Who makes the decisions in the church? Are they qualified to make decisions? How are the decisions made?
2. Ministry operation. How are the leaders selected? Are ministries evaluated periodically? Are new ministries added as needed? Are ministries terminated when no longer needed?

The organism aspect of the church has to do with its life and ministry. Are the people growing in their Christian life? Are they having daily Bible reading? Are they sharing with others what the Lord is teaching them? Are they having times of effective prayer? Are family relationships being built around the principles of Scripture? Are they applying Scripture to their personal lives? Are the sermons life-related? Are the Sunday school and other ministries meeting the needs of the people?

It is natural and essential for a living church to be a growing church. The redevelopment pastor must understand the dual nature of the church and how to set the stage for growth and thus halt the decline.

Sometimes this dual nature of the church can be self-destructing because the organization can choke out the organism, or the organism can resist organization. In the church there must be a balance between the organization and the organism if there is to be healthy growth.

My son, Stephen, taught me this important lesson through the life he lives. Stephen has cerebral palsy and is wheelchair-bound. In a layman's medical perspective, the human body has these same two functions as the body of Christ. There is the organizational function (the human skeleton) and the organism function (the human tissue, flesh, organs, etc.). Having a skeleton without the rest would be death; and having a living organism without the skeleton to hold them all in place would be equally disastrous. And in order to be effective, the growth of both the human body and the body of Christ must be balanced in organization and organism. Like some other children with cerebral palsy, sometimes Stephen's bones grow more rapidly than the rest of his body and he experiences pain as the muscles and skin are stretched to their maximum, sometimes necessitating corrective surgery. At other times his muscles and skin grow faster than his bone structure and then he is unable to move his arms or legs to the degree he would like. It is only when the growth of the skeleton matches the growth of the other body tissue that he can function as he wants.

Nehemiah probably did not have a sign on his office door that read "Redevelopment Pastor." Yet this man, perhaps more than any other in Scripture, demonstrates specific qualities that should be present in a redevelopment pastor. These qualities will be discussed in our study of Nehemiah's personal life and his ministry.

How Churches Grow

The third and last term needing to be defined is *growth in the ministry*. When speaking of growth in the ministry, it must be done so in terms of three interrelated areas: numerical growth, spiritual growth and organic growth (growth in the emergence of leadership from within the group). These are interrelated because one cannot occur consistently without the other two. If growth does occur in one area to the exclusion of growth in the other areas, the results will be short-lived.

Scripture refers to the local church as being the visible expression of the body of Christ, and in the analogy of a human body, it is natural for it to grow in these three ways also. As a body matures, it grows physically, mentally, socially and spiritually. Certain organs become activated as the body matures and they begin to function with maturity. It is not natural for a human body to grow physically, but not mentally. Neither is it natural for the human body to grow mentally, but not develop the physical functions related to adult life. And so on the comparisons could go. Just as a healthy human body experiences balanced growth, the body of Christ must have balanced growth numerically, spiritually and in the emergence of new leadership.

It is natural for the human body to grow when it is fed a nutritious diet in combination with measures of sleep and exercise. When it is free of disease and receives the necessary ingredients the human body *will* grow. It is also true that it is natural for a church to grow, providing it is free from the diseases of disunity and carnal self-will. When the life of the church centers around the spiritual basics of the Bible, prayer, fellowship and witnessing, and when the people live in obedience to the Lord, exercising their spiritual gifts and are responsible members of the church, then it *must* grow also.

When pastors today want to see growth in these areas, they may attend a leadership seminar, a church growth workshop or watch a video series on management. Nehemiah had no such options. But he did have an unshakable commitment to live and lead in total dependence upon the Lord. Nehemiah's account of how he brought numerical, spiritual and organic growth to a declining ministry provides the framework for you to do the same in your church.

Chapter 2

Nehemiah—A Man of Vision

[1:1–11]

No pastor will be able to impact his world for Jesus Christ unless he is able to see what others do not see; that is, he must be a man of vision. He must be like Moses, who "persevered because he saw him who is invisible" (Hebrews 11:27). Or, like Abraham who "was looking forward to the city with foundations, whose architect and builder is God" (11:10). Or, like Elisha, who was able to see what his servant could not see—the protection of the host of heaven (2 Kings 6:13–17). A man of faith must also be a man of vision.

Vision is not just something one develops in one's own mind—it is something that originates in the heart of the Lord Jesus and is revealed to the one whom He desires to carry out His plan. Being a man of vision meant that Nehemiah's walk with God was so intimate he could discern what the Lord wanted done in Jerusalem, and more specifically what He wanted Nehemiah to do personally.

Who Was This Man Nehemiah?

Not very much is known about the background of Nehemiah. He is introduced to us simply as the "son of Hacaliah" (Nehemiah 1:1), and there is not much known about him either. Nehemiah is similar to Elijah who merely appears

11

on the scene as God's man for the hour. All we do know about Nehemiah comes from the book he wrote and the historical, archaeological record of the days in which he lived.

There are, however, at least three assumptions we can make regarding Nehemiah's background:

1. He was born during the Babylonian captivity. The Jews were taken captive from 605 B.C. to 586 B.C.; Nehemiah's group went back to Jerusalem in 446 B.C., and he was in Jerusalem 12 years before returning to Babylon. Nehemiah was either born during the captivity, or he was at least 152 years old when he returned to the palace after rebuilding the wall at Jerusalem! Though there does not seem to be any record of Nehemiah's age, it is my personal opinion that Nehemiah was at least 40 to 50 years old when he began to rebuild the walls of Jerusalem.

2. Nehemiah rose to a position of eminence in the court (1:11), so he must have had some background in royal service. Daniel 1:3–4 gives us some detail on how those in royal service were selected in Babylon:
   - They had to be children of royalty or the noble people of the country. This probably stems from the thought that those in the upper classes of society are of greater leadership potential and have a greater capacity for knowledge.
   - They had to be physically healthy, socially adaptable, intelligent, able to reason and have an understanding of the sciences.
   - They also had to possess the psychological and emotional stability necessary to stand in positions of the palace and not become intimidated by the situation.
   - And finally, they had to have the capacity to learn a foreign language and speak it fluently.

3. Nehemiah's family must have come from Jerusalem since he referred to Jerusalem as the city "where my

fathers are buried" (2:5). This would have added to
his desire to return to Jerusalem and to rebuild the
walls and encourage God's people.

With the above assumptions about Nehemiah's background, it is most likely that Nehemiah's father and
grandfather were either in royal service or were prominent
men of Jerusalem.

One thing is certain in a careful study of the life of
Nehemiah–he was a man of vision. He had the ability to look
beyond the ruins of Jerusalem and see what the Lord God
wanted to bring into being. He could look beyond his plush
palace job and see the spiritual rewards of going to Jerusalem
to rebuild the wall and encourage God's people. He could
look beyond the discouragement of the people and see them
living in the joy of the Lord. He could look beyond a temple
in disarray and see a living, dynamic ministry.

The Development of Vision

The most familiar verse in the Scriptures regarding vision
is Proverbs 29:18: "Where there is no revelation (*vision*, KJV),
the people cast off restraint; but blessed is he who keeps the
law." Here, vision is seen as something God is able to reveal
to a believer who is living in fellowship with Him. It is a picture
of what God desires His people to do in order to fulfill His
perfect will. This revelation comes from God's heart to the
heart of a believer living in obedience to Him and is something he would never have otherwise known. (See 1 Samuel
3:1; Psalm 89:19; Isaiah 29:7; Jeremiah 14:14; and Ezekiel
12:22–24, 27.)

It follows, then, that if there is no governing revelation
from the Lord Jesus, the people will be out of control and
running wild. On the other hand, peace, joy and purpose in
living come from knowing the Lord Jesus through His Word
and living in obedience to its principles.

If we put all of these factors together, we can see why
Nehemiah made such an impact upon his time for God.
Proverbs 29:18 could be paraphrased like this:

When people walk after the desires of their own hearts and do not earnestly seek the Lord in an intimate relationship, He is not able to reveal to them what He wants to be done or what He wants them to do. As a result, the people have no purpose in living, no guidelines, no restraints, and they go in several different directions at once. Because of this lack of a defined purpose, they become discouraged and want to give up; they become exhausted. On the other hand, if they walk in God's ways they find purpose in living and experience joy in the Lord.

Nehemiah walked in a close relationship with the Lord, and God revealed His purposes for Nehemiah's life. With this singleness of purpose and his close walk with the Lord God, Nehemiah made a powerful impact upon his world because he was a man of vision.

How does the Lord God reveal His will to His people as they live in obedience to Him?

How It Happened with Nehemiah

One day while in the palace, Nehemiah heard one of his brethren speaking to another person. For some reason, Nehemiah asked them about things in general and more specifically about the conditions in Jerusalem. The one whom Nehemiah questioned was called Hanani, "one of my brothers" (Nehemiah 1:2). This does not necessarily mean Hanani was a blood relative; it could be a reference to the camaraderie of people with like national backgrounds who meet in a foreign land.

Hanani was one of the priests who evidently returned with Zerubbabel on the first return (cf. Ezra 2:37 and 10:20). After he returned to Jerusalem following the captivity or while he was in Babylon, Hanani married a foreign woman. Under Ezra's direction, Hanani was one of the men who promised to put away his foreign wife and make a new commitment to the Lord God. Hanani was probably in Shushan to give a report to the king regarding the progress of the rebuilding of the temple. The questions Nehemiah asked Hanani revolved around two areas: the condition of the people in Jerusalem and the condition of the city itself.

We can only speculate as to why Nehemiah was prompted to ask about Jerusalem and the conditions of the people. Nehemiah should have been obedient to the Lord and left Babylon at the time of the original decree from Cyrus to rebuild Jerusalem (2 Chronicles 36:22, 23 and Ezra 1:1-4). Whatever the situation, it is evident that since the time of the decree of Cyrus to the time Nehemiah began to inquire about Jerusalem and the people, the Lord had been working in his heart and Nehemiah was more responsive to the Lord's promptings than he had been before. The Lord is a God of second chances. From that point on, God began to unfold His plan for Nehemiah's life one step at a time.

How does God reveal His plans and purposes to His people? As with Nehemiah, vision begins with an awareness of a need (Nehemiah 1:2-3). But how do we sort out the multitude of needs that we are exposed to in the Christian life? Here is where the closeness of one's walk with the Lord becomes evident.

Prayer Reveals God's Plan

As we pray about needs, the Lord God impresses us about those we can become involved in by moving us emotionally (1:4). That is, He allows certain needs to filter down from the head to the heart, through prayer.

From the dates given in Nehemiah 1:1 and 2:1, we see that Nehemiah prayed concerning the matter for at least four months. The month *Kislev* would correspond to our November/December time period; the month *Nisan* would correspond to our March/April time.

Also, there is the element of specific prayer; those needs for which we are genuinely concerned become matters for earnest prayer (1:4ff.).

Finally, at some point in our prayers for a certain need, the Lord takes the request that we have offered up to Him and returns it to us as a responsibility in which we are to become actively involved (1:11ff.). As Nehemiah prayed for four months over the needs that he heard about, God impressed upon him the need for his personal involvement. Continued prayer on a matter will do that. It helps us to bring the matter into a much clearer focus than before and enables us to see what specific part the Lord would have us play in the answer to the prayer we offered.

Through this process of becoming aware of a need, being moved emotionally because of the need, taking it to the Lord in prayer and becoming personally and actively involved, the Lord reveals a vision to His people regarding what He wants accomplished.

The Need of the Hour

The redevelopment pastor needs to be a man of vision for two main reasons:

1. He must see the mind of God if the ministry is to grow, since there is often nothing else to see. In a declining ministry there is only the "rubble"—facilities in disrepair, people discouraged and without hope for the future and a ministry that is dying. If the redevelopment pastor is not a man of vision, he will soon become discouraged and end up just like the rest of his people.
2. He must sense what God wants to do in a declining ministry before he can lead the people in doing it. If he does not have any sense of direction from the Lord God, he will never be able to turn the declining ministry around and bring about lasting growth, nor will he be able to lead the people in a corporate, dynamic relationship with the Lord God.

Nehemiah was a man of vision. Every pastor, especially a redevelopment pastor, must also be a man of vision if he is going to turn a declining ministry into a living testimony for the Lord Jesus Christ.

Chapter 3

The Spiritual Life of a Leader

[1:4–11]

One of the pitfalls of being a spiritual leader is that in the process we can unintentionally neglect our own spiritual life. Jerry Mapstone, a district superintendent and former director of church growth with The Christian and Missionary Alliance, relates that almost every difficulty involving church leadership is due in large measure to the neglect of the leader's spiritual life disciplines.

Nehemiah was able to be used of the Lord God to rebuild the wall, encourage God's people and reestablish God's testimony in Jerusalem because he had a living, dynamic spiritual life. Like others before him, Nehemiah had learned how to live a godly life in a pagan land. Joseph, Moses, Daniel and Samuel are a few who grew up in the midst of an adverse spiritual environment and yet became godly men. There were several factors evident in Nehemiah's life that enabled him to live for the Lord and become an effective leader—his knowledge of the Scriptures, his personal prayer life, his exercise of the discipline of fasting and his reputation with those around him.

The Leader and His Knowledge of the Word

One of the first things that characterized Nehemiah's

spiritual life was his knowledge of the Word. He knew that Israel's captivity by the Babylonians was a result of their failure as a nation to obey the conditional promises of the Scriptures. In Nehemiah 1:7–9, he told the Lord in prayer how His people had known the commandments that He had given to Moses, but that they had been disobedient as a nation and were suffering the consequences; God had been faithful to His Word, but His people had not. Nehemiah also claimed the promise of God that if the Israelites would return to the Lord in true repentance that God would lead them back to the land of His promise.

The Word and Prayer

Nehemiah's knowledge of God's Word is evident in his prayer (1:4–11). His mind was so filled with the Scriptures that when he went to prayer, he based his petitions upon the promises of God. His prayer contains several quotes which Nehemiah evidently made from memory from five Old Testament books. Nehemiah not only spent time reading the Scriptures, but he had committed much of them to memory— so much that when he went to prayer, it was natural for him to pray in terms of the promises of God. One of the means of adding spiritual power to our prayers as well is to claim the promises of God as the basis for our petitions to Him.

Nehemiah's Prayer of 1:4–11

Nehemiah's Prayer	Scripture Verses Quoted
Nehemiah 1:5	Leviticus 26:42, 45
	Deuteronomy 4:31; 5:10; 7:9
Nehemiah 1:6	Leviticus 26:40
	1 Kings 8:29
	2 Chronicles 6:20, 38–40
Nehemiah 1:7	Leviticus 26:46
	2 Chronicles 6:36–37
Nehemiah 1:8	Leviticus 26:33
	Deuteronomy 4:27
Nehemiah 1:9	Deuteronomy 30:1–5
	2 Chronicles 7:14
Nehemiah 1:10	Deuteronomy 9:29

Nehemiah's Prayer	*Scripture Verses Quoted*
Nehemiah 1:11	*1 Kings 8:30*
	2 Chronicles 6:21; 7:15 [1]

The Word and Revival

A second outcome regarding Nehemiah's knowledge of the Scriptures was his desire for revival to come to God's people. Nehemiah knew that if revival was to come to Jerusalem it would come through the cleansing power of the Word of God (Ephesians 5:26) and a new commitment to live by the Scriptures. Chuck Swindoll said it well: "In every genuine revival in history, two major thrusts have always appeared. First, there has always been proclamation of the Bible, God's Word; second, there has always been the responsive mobilization of the believers, God's people."[2]

Nehemiah knew that when true revival takes place in the hearts of God's people, two elements are always present:

1. There is a strong adherence to the Bible as the infallible Word of God. This message is preached in the pulpits and believed in the hearts of all who hear.
2. There is the mobilization of all God's people into ministry, each using their gifts, talents, and abilities in service for the Lord Jesus.

In chapters 8–10, Nehemiah led the people through a process of making that new commitment. First he brought Ezra to lead them in the Scripture reading and personal applications. Next, because the Lord brought conviction upon their hearts through the exposure to the Scriptures, they went to prayer, and ended by making a new commitment to the Lord God. This commitment was expressed in a written document and was signed by those who wanted to live on a higher plane with the Lord God at the center of their lives. And Nehemiah's name stood at the top of the list—right where a leader's name should appear (10:1). These steps in the process of revival will be studied in greater detail in later chapters.

The Leader and His Prayer Life

A second aspect of Nehemiah's spiritual life that is evident in his book is his effective, fervent prayer life (James 5:16).

An effective prayer life completes the communication cycle with the Lord God. He speaks to His people through the Scriptures and His people, in turn, speak to Him in prayer. Any spiritual leader who seeks to lead God's people in any capacity needs to keep in constant communication with the One whom he serves. A soldier in the midst of a war who is separated from his base unit soon learns that his radio is an extremely important piece of equipment. Through it he can talk to his home unit and his home unit can talk to him. As Christians living in an alien world that is in the hand of the evil one (1 John 5:19), communication is essential, and more so for those in positions of spiritual leadership.

Prayer in Adversity

Another facet of Nehemiah's prayer life is seen in how he reacted to adversity. Nehemiah's first response to discouraging information and circumstances was to take the matter to the Lord in prayer. Several times Nehemiah would come face to face with a situation in which he could not see any human possibilities. It was then that he would go to prayer, knowing that nothing is too hard for God (Jeremiah 32:27). When Nehemiah first heard of the broken-down condition of Jerusalem and the discouragement of the people, he went to prayer (Nehemiah 1:4–11). He knew it was often at the point of man's greatest failures that the power and glory of God came into action in response to the prayers of His people. When he was questioned by the king concerning his fallen countenance, Nehemiah went to prayer (2:4). When the enemy stirred up people to hurl accusations and innuendoes at Nehemiah, he went to prayer (4:4–6, 8–9; 5:19; 6:9, 14). No matter what adversity came to Nehemiah, he prayed.

It is important for the Christian, and especially the redevelopment pastor, to learn to respond to adversity first with prayer. It should be noted here that we speak of adversity in the sense that we did not cause it, but that it was placed upon us, not as a result of our own actions or inactions. I have noticed that Christians will respond to adversity in one of three ways:

- outward in anger toward others or things;
- inward in bitterness by withdrawing from others;
- upward in trust in a sovereign God.

It is only through the third response that we will be able to gain the blessing that the Lord God designed in our experiencing the adversity.

Scriptures on Adversity

There are two Scriptures that come to mind in responding to adversity:

1. Romans 8:28—a verse that is often misunderstood and misapplied. This verse promises that all things work together for good, but not automatically. It is only for those who love God and who are part of the called according to His purposes. If my response to adversity does not reflect my trust and love for the Lord God, then He cannot use it for my good. This verse is like baking a cake "from scratch." Taken individually, the ingredients are not very tasty, but when added together in the right proportions and popped into the oven, they make a delicious cake. Often the "ingredients" of life taken individually do not make sense or seem profitable to us. But taken in the right proportions with other life ingredients, including the heat of adversity, they all work together to form new things in our lives.

2. Genesis 50:20—where Joseph reaffirms his trust in a sovereign God. Joseph knew that even though the adversity was a result of the actions of others, that God was the one who governed his life and that if God so directed adversity to be a part of his life, then God

would, and did, use it for His ultimate purposes for Joseph's life.

Many of the lessons that are presented in this book are lessons that were begun as a result of personal adversity. The redevelopment pastor must learn that when adversity strikes, prayer must be his first response. By doing so, he affirms that God will use it to develop Christlike character, give direction to his ministry or teach new insights into the Scriptures that could not be otherwise understood. But more than that, it is affirming his trust in a sovereign God whom he serves in the work to which he has been called.

Not only did Nehemiah have an effective, fervent prayer life personally, he desired that the people live in dependence upon the Lord as well. In Nehemiah 9:1–38, he wanted to lead the people into a new depth of fellowship with the Lord in their own prayer life.

Nehemiah knew what it was to have a balanced life in regard to the Word of God and prayer, and that is what he wanted to instill in the hearts of the people of God. He knew that if believers gave themselves to the study of the Word of God, but not to prayer, their lives would soon become filled with pride and their knowledge of the Word would lack experience. On the other hand, if believers gave themselves to prayer, but not to the study of the Word of God, they would soon become ingrown in their perspective and unbalanced in their understanding of what the Lord God is doing in the world.

Though he probably did not lead the people personally in the prayer recorded in chapter 9, the desire of Nehemiah's heart was that the people be led in a corporate prayer experience that would continue on in their own lives.

The Leader and the Discipline of Fasting

There is a third area of Nehemiah's spiritual life that is exemplary. Nehemiah was one who practiced the spiritual discipline of fasting. There are three types of fasting which are described in the Scriptures.

First, the *normal fast* is characterized by abstaining from food only, not drink. An example of the normal fast is seen in Matthew 4:2. After Jesus had fasted for 40 days, the Bible records that He was hungry; nothing was mentioned about His being thirsty. Since pains from thirst are often more intense and come before the pains from hunger, the verse suggests that this fast was an abstaining from food, but not from water.

Second, the *absolute fast* involves abstaining from both food and drink. There are at least five instances in the Scriptures where people are said to have abstained from both eating and drinking for an extended period of time.

Moses underwent an absolute fast for 40 days while he was on Mount Sinai talking with God and receiving the Ten Commandments (Deuteronomy 9:9). That fast itself was supernatural because it was so long. After Moses came down from the mountain and saw the people living in sin, he broke the tablets of stone bearing the Ten Commandments. He then returned to the presence of God on the mountain and spent an additional 40 days in absolute fasting (9:10–18).

Elijah also had a supernatural 40-day fast as recorded in First Kings 19:1–8. After the angel fed him twice in the wilderness, he got up and went for 40 days and nights in the strength of that nourishment.

It should be noted that both instances of 40-day absolute fasts with Moses and Elijah were supernatural. Scripture indicates that absolute fasts normally last much shorter—one to three days at the most as indicated by the instances of Ezra, Esther and Paul.

In Ezra 10:1ff, Ezra wept and cast himself down before the Lord in confession of sin for the Israelites because the men had married foreign, heathen women. Ezra then fasted and called for an assembly in three days of all Israel regarding the matter. The implication was that Ezra prayed and fasted for those three days on behalf of the people to come and deal with this sin.

When Queen Esther found out that wicked Haman had plotted to murder the Jews of the land, she requested that

her uncle Mordecai join her and her servants in an absolute
fast for three days and nights (Esther 4:1–17). This fast was
for her to gain approval to come into the king's presence. If
such approval was not granted she could be put to death.

A third instance of an absolute fast is during the time of
Paul's conversion (Acts 9:1–9). After his experience with the
Lord Jesus Christ on the road to Damascus, Paul was led away
blind to the house of Judas where he fasted for three days.

The last type of fasting that the Bible records is that of the
partial fast. Daniel tells us that "I ate no choice food; no meat
or wine touched my lips; and I used no lotions at all until
three weeks were over" (Daniel 10:3). Daniel did not abstain
from food altogether; he merely restricted himself from
partaking of certain foods.

Each of these three types of fasting is an equally spiritual
discipline into which the Lord may lead His people.

It is not determined what type of fasting that Nehemiah
undertook, but it was probably either the normal fast or the
absolute fast since it was for "certain days."

Why Fast?

The purposes of fasting are not to "twist God's arm" or to
impress Him with our devotion. There are several reasons for
us to pursue fasting:[3]

1. To set aside a number of uninterrupted hours to talk
    with the Lord and experience a special time of in-
    timate fellowship with Him. Sometimes in our
    everyday schedule we can get so busy that it is of great
    benefit to relax in the company of the Lord Jesus
    Christ. In Matthew 5:1, the Lord Jesus was in the
    midst of a busy ministry schedule. In the middle of it
    all He called His disciples to come spend some time
    alone with Him, away from the multitudes, so He
    could teach them privately. I find that when the
    pressures of the ministry and the demands upon my
    time become the greatest, I also need to schedule a
    time to be alone with the Lord to let Him teach me

privately and refresh my spirit. I find that these times alone with Him are so important that the only alternative to coming apart with the Lord is "coming apart at the seams." These times of prayer and fasting help us place the focus of our hearts upon the Lord Jesus so we can gain a clearer perspective of Him and our relationship to Him.

2. The need for personal cleansing. Prayer and fasting play a significant role in taking the mental and physical focus off of food and placing it upon the Lord Jesus Christ. In doing so we deny the body and mind in favor of feeding the spirit and this often results in a measure of increased sanctification.

3. There are times in our lives when personal crises call for prayer and fasting to help us deal with them. When major doubts, persistent temptations, failing interpersonal relationships or times of confusion come, we need to set aside time for fasting and prayer.

4. At times when we feel our ministry is on the spiritual decline and we need new direction, or we desire new power in ministry, or we feel the need to find a new method or new insight, an unhurried period with the Lord provides an opportunity for Him to deal with us in an unusual way.

5. There are instances when we need an unhurried block of time with the Lord for our intercession for others. As the prayer list grows and the work schedule becomes heavier, we may find we neglect or abbreviate our intercession for the important needs of others. This is not a deliberate neglect, it's just that our schedule has crowded out longer periods of quality prayer time. A prolonged time of prayer and fasting enables us to get away from our schedule, spend a greater amount of time in prayer and center our attention for long periods of time upon the needs of others. "It takes more than a little short prayer to get away from our own selfishness. We have, each of us, so many needs that we will not do our duty in praying

for others unless we take an extended time for it, unless we really wait before God long enough to get out of our selfishness and get victory over our own immediate needs."[4]

6. While seeking guidance, especially when facing a major decision. Then the Lord can bring all the factors into focus from His perspective. Fasting is also a means through which the Lord can give us His direction for our life and ministry. As we see in Acts 13:1-3, it was while the leaders of the church at Antioch were praying and fasting that the Holy Spirit was able to give them clear direction for the ministry He was calling Barnabas and Saul to do. Fasting does not give us better access to the Lord God—the blood of the Lord Jesus Christ has ensured that open access. Instead, fasting provides the Lord a better access to our hearts.

Seeking the Lord's direction in this way can be done on an individual basis or by groups and organizations. When planning for the future, it is well to spend an extended time, without distractions, seeking to know His plan. First Corinthians 1:9 tells us that we were called into the fellowship of the Lord Jesus Christ; times of fasting, coupled with prayer, greatly enhance that fellowship with Him. Nehemiah fasted for the condition of God's testimony and for His people in Jerusalem (Nehemiah 1:4). The redevelopment pastor will also know many times in which he will feel the great need for prayer and fasting for his own life and for the lives of the people whom he serves.

The Life of the Leader as Seen by Others

A fourth aspect of Nehemiah's spiritual life was his good testimony with those outside the family of God's people. In First Timothy 3:1-7, Paul listed several qualities to look for in the life of a man who was to be appointed to spiritual leadership within the church. One of those character qualities was that he have a good testimony before those in the world. The Christian, and especially the Christian leader, must not the friendship of the world, nor love the world (1 John 2:15–17); but at the same time, he cannot afford to be antagonistic toward the lost world whom he serves as Christ's ambassador (2 Corinthians 5:20). "In any dealings with the authorities or with non-Christians generally, the church would start with a disadvantage if its spokesman did not command respect. The text does not mean that the (spiritual leader) should be popular with the outsiders because he is 'one of the boys.' As a general rule even unbelieving men can recognize character when they see it."[5] The world may not like what we stand for, but they must not find deception in our lives.

Further, Nehemiah was a trusted servant of the king. The position Nehemiah held as the king's cupbearer was one of great responsibility and he had proved himself to be trustworthy in the king's eyes. The king's cupbearer was not only the head of all of the household servants, but he also tasted everything that the king would eat and drink before the king did. Being the king's cupbearer "gave him the opportunity of being frequently with the king; and to be in such a place of trust, he must be in the king's confidence. No Eastern potentate would have a cupbearer with whom he could not trust his life, poison being frequently administered in this way."[6] Nehemiah had an impeccable testimony before his unsaved employer, the king.

If a pastor is bi-vocational, he must be careful to have a testimony in his secular job as being a good, trustworthy employee. His employer and fellow employees may not be willing to receive a salvation message, but they must not be able to discount that message because of the life of the one giving the message.

In Ezra 4:6–16, King Artaxerxes had stopped the work on the wall at Jerusalem because he heard reports that once the walls were repaired the Jews would rebel against his reign. These reports were believable, especially because the king knew that the Jews had a history of rebellion against authority (4:19–20).

Nehemiah was aware of all this, so when he told the king

of his desire to rebuild the wall and encourage God's people, he did not mention the name of the city (Nehemiah 2:5–8). He knew that the name "Jerusalem" would only stir up unnecessary thoughts of hesitancy. He also knew that the king's letter to stop the work contained a provision that work on the city could resume at a later date if another letter from the king so directed (Ezra 4:21). Tactfully, Nehemiah made his appeal for such an additional directive from the king so that it would not appear as if the king had changed his mind. Though King Artaxerxes knew of the Jews' rebellious history, he trusted Nehemiah enough to let him return and rebuild the city. The testimony that Nehemiah had as a trusted servant outweighed the rebelliousness of the Jews in the mind of the king.

It is also important for the Christian leader to exercise tact, as Nehemiah did, in carrying out his God-given responsibilities. This is especially important when a church is involved with a building program such as Nehemiah was. Zoning variances and building permits have been slowed down considerably because the pastor or church leaders did not exercise tact with the city planning commission or the zoning board. Pastors and Christian leaders must exercise tact when dealing with unsaved governmental officials, or else unnecessary obstacles will be placed before the work that the Lord has called us to do.

There is another aspect of Nehemiah's testimony with those outside the family of God's people. He was sensitive to the feelings of the king and he spoke in terms that the king could understand. Because the king was not a child of God, Nehemiah spoke of Jerusalem as being the city "where my fathers are buried" something to which the king could relate. The king was a worshiper of ancestry and the city of his fathers' tombs was a sacred place for him—he immediately knew what Nehemiah was talking about. "The tombs of the dead were sacred among the ancients, and nothing could appear to them more detestable than disturbing the ashes or remains of the dead. Nehemiah knew that in mentioning this circumstance he should strongly interest the feelings of the Persian king."[7]

It is easy for Christians to talk in terms that are well known among believers, but that are totally foreign to the unsaved world such as "born again," "saved," "sanctification" and "glory." The Christian leader who will be effective in winning the world for Jesus Christ and making an impact upon society for Him must learn, as Nehemiah did, to talk in terms that the world understands without compromising the message.

A final aspect regarding Nehemiah's testimony with those who were outside the family of God concerned his word. Nehemiah was a man of his word. While the king considered granting Nehemiah permission to return to Jerusalem, he asked how long it would take Nehemiah to complete the task (Nehemiah 2:6). Here is an excellent example of the combination of faith and works, as discussed in chapter 9. While Nehemiah was praying for the four months prior to the king's questioning, he was also planning out his strategy. And he had planned it so well that he even developed a timetable and a list of materials that he would require! He was so sure that the Lord God would answer his prayer, that he counted it to be so and planned accordingly while he waited patiently upon the Lord for His timing in the unfolding of His will. Nehemiah gave the king a specific time when he would return and he kept his word (see also 13:6).

It is so important for Christians working with those in the world to be known as people who keep their word—to be honest. If those in the world even suspect an element of dishonesty in the life or message of the Christian, they will totally discount the Christian testimony we want to present. We need to remember that we are "Christ's ambassadors" (2 Corinthians 5:20) and our credibility in the world must be crystal clear.

Bringing It Close to Home

Nehemiah was aware that there was a cause and effect between one's relationship to the Lord and the functions of life (Nehemiah 1:4-11). When a person or nation walks in obedience to the Lord there is blessing, but when a person or nation turns in disobedience and does not follow the Lord whole-heartedly, there follows chastisement. Revival is walking in obedience to the Lord and living in His blessing.

Nehemiah knew that it was not enough for him to rebuild the wall and the city. It was not for lack of military might that Jerusalem fell in the first place. Nehemiah also wanted to bring revival to God's people—a rebuilding of the testimony of the living, dynamic God in the lives of His people who were to be His advertisements in the world. As Paul wrote in Ephesians 6:12, the battles of life for God's people may be manifested in the physical realm, but the real battles take place in the spiritual realm. More than anything else, the people needed revival in their hearts.

After he rebuilt the wall, Nehemiah devoted his time to train faithful men for positions of service (chapter 7) and to bring about a revival in the lives of people (chapters 8–10).

There are at least four reasons why the redevelopment pastor must guard his personal relationship with the Lord because of its effect upon his ministry:

1. As is the case of any spiritual leader, the relationship with the Lord must be a foundational basis for his life and ministry. He must guard against becoming so busy serving the Lord that he has no time to have communion with the Lord. He must remember that ministry is the overflow of communion with the Lord and if there is no time to have that communion with Him, there will be no lasting effects of his ministry.

2. The redevelopment pastor must remember that cultivating his spiritual life is necessary to maintain a clear focus on the work the Lord has called him to do. As mentioned in chapter 2, vision initially comes out of one's walk with the Lord as He reveals what He desires to be done in a particular place. Unless one maintains that same intimate walk with the Lord, he will not continue to have the clear focus of vision that he had in the first place. In a declining ministry it is so easy to start with a clear vision that becomes foggy

in a very short time if we are not careful. From personal experience I can attest how easy it is to become embroiled over the multitude of problems that exist in declining churches, or with the person or small group within the church that does not want the work to grow, or that person who is against you no matter what you do or say. It is the personal, daily walk with the Lord Jesus that keeps everything in sharp focus. It is not an optional discipline, it is vital. The spiritual life of the redevelopment pastor is something that must be carefully guarded.

3. The spiritual life of the redevelopment pastor is necessary for his own encouragement in the trials of the work. Once he has arrived on the scene and begun his ministry, the enemy will raise up all sorts of discouraging people and discouraging situations in order to bring him down to the pit of despair. The enemy, Satan, does not want the declining ministry to become a growing ministry and he knows that the redevelopment pastor is the key to the transition. If the enemy can get the redevelopment pastor discouraged, the vision will be lost and the whole ministry will suffer for it.

4. Healthy spiritual development keeps life's rewards in perspective. Usually there is not the financial backing available to a redevelopment pastor as there is to pastors in other ministries. One of the deceptions of the enemy is to keep reminding the redevelopment pastor that if he were in some other type of ministry he could be earning much more money and be a better provider for his family. Although there needs to be adequate financial support for the redevelopment pastor, he usually ends up with "too much month at the end of the money." One thing he needs to bear in mind is that the judgment seat of Christ is coming and the Lord Jesus will then reward the faithful service of His people.

Chapter 4

The Secular Life of a Leader

[1:11]

When we examine the life and ministry of Nehemiah, we must keep in mind that though he was a man of God, he was not a priest or professional spiritual leader. He was a royal servant, a political governor, sent on a mission by the king.

In Nehemiah 1:11, Nehemiah tells us that he was the king's cupbearer. James Orr notes that the king's cupbearer was

> . . . an officer of high rank at ancient oriental courts, whose duty it was to serve the wine at the king's table. On account of the constant fear of plots and intrigues, a person must be regarded as thoroughly trustworthy to hold this position. He must guard against poison in the king's cup, and was sometimes required to swallow some of the wine before serving it. His confidential relations with the king often endeared him to his sovereign and also gave him a position of great influence.[1]

If, when the cupbearer ate the food and drank the drink, he did not die, the royal family knew they were safe to enjoy the meal.

Because of his position, the king's cupbearer was often a

personal confidant to the king. The king trusted his cupbearer with his life and with the lives of his royal family. He
was also, of necessity, a person of great influence with the
king. The king would listen to what his cupbearer had to say
and would give it his careful consideration. Thus, the cupbearer was more than a servant; he was often a political
advisor as well.

In Nehemiah's case, his loyalty to and interest in the king
whom he served went beyond the normal servant relationship. In Nehemiah 2:6, he tells us that he was serving the king
and the queen was beside the king. "As the Persian monarchs
did not admit their wives to be present at their state festivals,
this must have been a private occasion."[2] Nehemiah's service
went beyond the professional level to the personal level; he
was genuinely interested in the total well-being of the one
whom he served.

The redevelopment pastor must also move beyond the
professional level to the personal level; he must get to know
the people he has come to serve. No pastor can preach to
people he does not know. The redevelopment pastor above
all others cannot afford to sit in his office, develop sermons
and strategies and expect the people to become excited about
their church and help him rebuild it. He must also develop
personal relationships with the people of the church and
demonstrate a genuine interest in their welfare.

Preparation for Ministry

The term "cupbearer" is used in other passages in the Old
Testament Scriptures (1 Kings 10:5, 2 Chronicles 9:4 and
Genesis 40, 41). From these three passages of Scripture, as
well as the book of Nehemiah, we can study the duties of a
cupbearer and see how the Lord God prepared Nehemiah
for his service by the training he received as a servant in the
king's palace. For instance, in Genesis 40:1, the one in this
position is called "the" cupbearer while in the verse following
(40:2) he is referred to as the "chief" cupbearer. All of this
seems to indicate that the position of cupbearer was one in
which the individual exercised authority over lesser servants

and had oversight of the domestic functions of the king's household. As the king's cupbearer, Nehemiah was the head of all the household servants. There he learned how to lead others in the work at hand and how to fulfill the desires of the one in authority over him.

Further, in First Kings 10:5 and Second Chronicles 9:4, the cupbearers were part of the picture with which Solomon presented to the Queen of Sheba in order to impress her—which indicates the position of a cupbearer was one of esteem and prominence in the king's service. One final note: because of Nehemiah's own personal wealth (Nehemiah 5:8, 10, 14, 17) we can assume that the position of a cupbearer was a financially profitable position.

God often uses a man's secular job to prepare him for a specific ministry in building his kingdom. "In a very simple but solemn manner, God had been quietly at work, chiseling and grinding to hone a man to do a job," Richard Seume writes of Nehemiah. "The axe was now sharpened; the instrument is ready for the task."[3] God trained Nehemiah in the palace of a king, then sent him on a divine mission to serve the King of kings.

Four Lessons

There were four lessons which Nehemiah learned in the palace:

1. Response to Authority

He learned how to respond to the authorities over him (Romans 13:1-7 and Matthew 8:5-10). In Luke 16:12, the Lord Jesus emphasizes the importance of learning how to respond to the authorities over us such as governmental officers, church leaders, employers and family heads. There he tells us that before a man can be *in* authority, he must first learn how to be *under* authority. No man can be an effective leader until he has first learned to be a servant. Neither can he expect others to respond to his authority if he himself is in rebellion against the authorities in his life.

While in the palace, Nehemiah learned to serve under the

authority of the king. The joy in serving others is experienced when we delight to carry out their desires as our own. Nehemiah had demonstrated his submission to the king's authority over him, not only developing trust in the king's mind so that he would be allowed to go, but also qualifying himself in the sight of God to be a leader of His people. One of the four major principles of stewardship that the Lord Jesus gave is "if you have not been trustworthy with someone else's property (submitting to his authority over you), who will give you property of your own (being in authority over others)?" (Luke 16:12).

2. Delegation of Jobs

Nehemiah learned to delegate jobs and to know what jobs cannot be delegated at all. When the person in the position of leadership fails to delegate some of his workload to his subordinates, it is detrimental both to him and to those who work under him.

The man in a place of leadership who fails to delegate is constantly enmeshed in a morass of secondary details that not only overburdens him, but deflects him from his primary responsibilities. He also fails to release the leadership potential of those under him. To insist on doing things oneself because it will be done better is not only a shortsighted policy but may be evidence of an unwarranted conceit.[4]

The redevelopment pastor must never forget that his calling is to equip the people for ministry, not to do the ministry all himself (Ephesians 4:11–12). Only a leader full of unhealthy pride thinks others cannot do it as well as he can, and therefore does not delegate part of his work responsibilities.

Nehemiah was responsible for all the domestic duties in the palace and was also head over all the other household servants. Thus in the palace he learned how to delegate responsibilities to others in order to get the job completed.

Think of what might have happened to Nehemiah if he had not learned how to delegate tasks to others. One thing for certain is that it would have taken him longer than 52 days to rebuild the walls of Jerusalem. He would not have become the esteemed leader that he did if he had not recognized his own limitations and the potential in others, and given them the opportunity to carry out part of the task which the Lord God had called him to accomplish.

On the other hand, a wise leader recognizes that there are also tasks which he cannot delegate. Others can have a part in their formulation, but they can never be turned over to subordinates completely. Ted Engstrom identifies some responsibilities that a leader cannot delegate:

> . . . setting objectives for the division or department for which he is responsible; building teamwork by organizing the work for maximizing coordination, communication and cooperation; coaching and developing subordinates to acquire knowledge and skill and to increase motivation and job satisfaction; setting individual goals on quantity, quality, costs, and time. Disciplinary matters also should never be delegated. Final authority in such matters must rest with the leader, because ultimate review of possible disciplinary action will be his anyway.[5]

When it came to handling certain aspects of the work in Jerusalem, Nehemiah knew that he must stand alone and shoulder the task himself.

3. Leader of People

Nehemiah also learned to lead people. Because he was the head of a number of palace servants, he learned the art of people handling.

Any leader leads from two basic stances: either he will be a goal/task oriented leader or he will be a people/social oriented leader. The best leader is one who can change from one type to the other and know when to change.

A leader has to bear in mind that he has a job to accomplish, a goal to be attained; but that he must enlist the help of other people and motivate them also to achieve the goal. That becomes the art of people management—an art at which

Nehemiah learned to function very well. In chapter six we will examine Nehemiah's leadership abilities in greater detail, but it must be remembered that those skills were perfected in the palace.

4. Attention to Details

Nehemiah had to learn to pay attention to the details of his appointed tasks. It is this quality of leadership that all leaders must learn: that of doing all things "as working for the Lord" (Colossians 3:23-24). For the Christian, doing all things as unto the Lord means going the extra mile. It means having a higher standard of excellence. It means carrying out each task as it if were to be observed or scrutinized by the Lord Jesus Himself, in every detail and motive.

While in secular college, I used to work with a man whose standard saying when he finished a job was, "Well, that's good enough for a town this size." I have met pastors of small churches who, although they do not say it, seem to have that same philosophy of ministry. But whatever ministry we are called to serve, the size of that ministry should not detract our attention from the One who called us to it. The same Lord is over the small ministry as any other ministry and He deserves nothing but our best in every detail.

Nehemiah learned to give attention to the details, or the little things of life. In Luke 16:10 and Song of Songs 2:15, Scripture gives us some important help regarding the leader's attention to the details of his efforts.

Luke 16:10 reminds us that we must demonstrate faithfulness to the Lord Jesus in the little things of life before He will trust us with greater things. In the life of the redevelopment pastor, this means that if he is not faithful in the little things of his own life, nor the little things of the struggling church, the Lord will not cause it to grow no matter what is done there.

In Song of Songs 2:15, the Scripture uses a little phrase, "the little foxes that ruin the vineyards." As the owner or caretaker looked out over his vineyard, it was easy to see the big foxes come in to eat the grapes and spoil the vines. These big foxes could be fought off, but the little foxes did not rustle the leaves when they entered the vineyard, so they were much harder to catch. These little foxes could come up under the vines, eat the grapes and destroy the vines without the people even knowing they were there. That is, unless they were diligent in keeping watch for "the little foxes that ruin the vineyards."

Often the devil knows he cannot trap a spiritual leader into the big sins of life (not that there is any difference in sin in God's eyes). The spiritual leader may not steal, murder, commit adultery, or things like that, so the devil will seek to ensnare the leader in the little things of life—a compromise here and a compromise there, a lie here, a deception there. A leader must learn to attend to the little things both of his own life and in the work to which he has been called.

The Secular Side of the Ministry

The secular activities of the redevelopment pastor must not be overlooked. No one can use one standard for one area of life and another standard for other areas of life. In Luke 2:52, the Scripture tells us that the Lord Jesus developed in wisdom (mental development) and in stature (physical development) and in favor with God (spiritual development) and man (social development). Each one of these four areas of personal development must be in balance with the others or they will make the person like a wheel with four uneven spokes. It will roll and carry a load, but the ride will be a rough one. Also, James 1:8 tells us further that, if we have one standard for one area of our life and a different standard for another area of our life, it will eventually make us unstable in all areas. The Christian, and especially the redevelopment pastor, must take care to lead a balanced life and have a testimony for the Lord Jesus in his whole life experience—spiritual as well as secular. The redevelopment pastor must be committed to having God's best in all the details of every aspect of his life and ministry—the sacred as well as the secular—for they all are part of one unit.

In addition to his preaching ability the redevelopment

pastor may need carpentry skills to build or remodel the physical facilities, and motivational skills to lead discouraged people into a dynamic testimony for the Lord Jesus Christ. The redevelopment pastor must at least have enough knowledge of these other skills to know what must be accomplished in order to turn the declining ministry around (or have quality men around him who possess these skills and are also committed to the pastor and to his vision). The use of these other skills will be discussed in greater detail in a later chapter.

As in all levels of spiritual leadership, there must be a commitment to excellence in both the sacred and the secular activities of the ministry if it is to bring lasting glory to the Lord God. Nehemiah learned this principle and demonstrated it in his life and ministry. Can the same be said of your ministry?

Chapter 5

The Leader and His Family Life

[2:8, 11–12]

Before we can look at Nehemiah's family life and see how it fits into his overall scheme of ministry, we need to answer a question held by some. Because it was generally held that male palace servants were also eunuchs, some would say that Nehemiah was, in fact, a eunuch and would not have been married at all—even though such an idea is neither supported nor inferred in the biblical record.

It is true that cupbearers were generally eunuchs. However, the word "eunuch" has a primary meaning and a secondary meaning, though the secondary meaning is the one that is thought of most readily. Of the Hebrew word for "eunuch" (*sarus*) the *Theological Wordbook of the Old Testament* records for us, "the noun, meaning (court) official, has its origin in the Akadian title (SARRI) 'the one of the (king's) head.' The meaning 'eunuch' arose with the practice of utilizing castrated men in key positions in the various nations of the near east."[1]

However, to say that because Nehemiah was an official of the palace he was an emasculated man ignores Nehemiah's understanding of the Word of God. Nehemiah knew the Scriptures and had committed much of it to memory, as we previously examined in chapter 3. He would have known that the law stated that no emasculated man could enter into the congregation of the Lord (Deuteronomy 23:1; Leviticus 21:16ff; 22:24). And knowing that, Nehemiah could not have participated in the worship of the Lord in the celebration of the completion of the walls and the restoration of temple services. Had Nehemiah been the emasculated man who some hold him to be, he would have violated the law that he loved so much in order to take part in the ceremonies of Nehemiah 8–12.

It is my belief that Nehemiah was an official of the king's court, but that he was also a married man with a family, even though he does not mention them in his book. It is of no particular significance that Nehemiah does not mention his family members; neither did he mention his parental background or any of the other details of his personal life. I believe Nehemiah was like many who are in a public ministry—they shield their family from the scrutiny of the public as much as they can.

Only One Hired per Family

When pastors, and redevelopment pastors as well, accept a call to a church, they need to ensure that the church's governing body recognizes that they have called *him*, and him alone; his wife is not a part of the agreement. Sometimes a church will feel as if they are calling the man to be their pastor and his wife to be his assistant. I know of no other profession where such demands are made on the part of a man's wife as there are in the pastorate. A surgeon's wife is not expected to assist her husband in surgery, nor is a lawyer's wife expected to go to court with her husband. If a plumber cannot make the service call, no one expects his wife to fill in for him.

Therefore, I believe, the pastor needs to make it clear to the church that calls him that he is to be their pastor and that his wife is his wife. She does not need to be the women's leader, the church musician or the children's worker. Her first responsibility is her husband and their family, and especially so if they have school-age children at home. The church that will understand this order will have a better pastor because of it. This is not to say that she cannot take an active part in the ministry, only that it is not to be expected of her merely because her husband is the pastor.

Nehemiah demonstrates in his book how the priorities of the man in full-time service to the Lord all fit together, the priority of the family being one that fits into the overall scheme of his life and ministry.

In the life of the redevelopment pastor, as with any Christian married man, the family must have its rightful priority or else the man is headed for danger. If his ministry is not being carried out in his family life, it will not happen in the life of the church either. The big difference is that he can be replaced in the church, but not in his family. In any ministry of the gospel, the real danger is for a man to set out to win the world for Christ and do a work for Him, but in the process lose his own family. All Christian workers, and especially those in full-time ministry, must give attention to the biblical order of their life priorities.

Three Myths Regarding the Family and the Ministry

1. "Ministry vs. family—that is, one must be sacrificed in order to do the other." Those who hold to this myth say that there is the constant tension between the family and the ministry and each is vying for the time of the one in the middle. But when a pastor recognizes the order of biblical priorities for his life, he will see that there is complete harmony between family and ministry. There is, in fact, no competition at all between the two. Nehemiah not only recognized the order of the biblical priorities for his life, but he demonstrated their order in his life and in his ministry.

2. "The quality of time spent with the family is more important than the quantity of time." But to set quality time in opposition with quantity time is like asking, "Is it more important to breathe in, or breathe out?" or "Which is more important, sales or service?" If one is going to continue to live, one must breathe in as well as breathe out. And if a business is to grow,

it must service what it sells. The spiritual leader cannot afford to set quantity time at odds with quality
time. He must invest a quantity of quality time with
his family if he will have an ongoing ministry with
eternal results.
3. "There is never enough time." The fact is, there will
always be enough time to do what we are supposed
to do in the will of God for our own life. Many times
the problem is not the lack of time, but the management of the time we have. The Lord has given
everyone the same amount of time each day and will
not overburden us with more than what He intends
for us to handle. However, we need to be sure that
we have our life priorities in order and that we are
not taking upon ourselves more than He has required
of us. It is when we do take upon ourselves more than
what He wants us to do that responsibilities and
priorities clash.

Nehemiah Masters the Myths

Here again, Nehemiah demonstrated how he looked after
the welfare of his family and, at times, even set aside his work
of ministry in order to be with his family and meet their needs.

When Nehemiah left the palace in Shushan to go to
Jerusalem, he made sure that the needs of his family were
planned out in just as much detail as he had planned out all
the other facets of the work. He wanted to keep the priorities
of his life in their correct biblical order right from the
beginning of this new work which the Lord had called him to
do. There are two ways in which Nehemiah demonstrated the
priority of his family in his life.

Providing for His Family

Nehemiah exercised care in making plans for the
provisions that his family would need for the trip and for their
new home in Jerusalem. In Nehemiah's request to go back to
Jerusalem to rebuild the walls and encourage the people, it
was important to him that the king send him and that he not

merely be allowed a leave of absence to go there on his own (Nehemiah 2:5). Nehemiah knew that if the king would send him that he would go as the governor of the city and would still be on the payroll as an official of the king. He knew he needed the income to support his family and so he requested that the king send him to Jerusalem to do the work the Lord had called him to do; and the king granted Nehemiah's request (2:6). Further, knowing the territory between Shushan and Jerusalem and the dangers it held, Nehemiah also requested letters from the king asking the governors of the city/states through which they must travel for safe passage through their land (2:7). I believe that Nehemiah was concerned about the safety of the travel for his family as well as for his own life. Evidently the king thought so as well, for he not only granted the request for the letters of conveyance, but also sent along a small army for their protection (2:9). In his request for supplies from the king, Nehemiah also requested enough materials so that he could build a house for himself (2:8). He knew that in going to a new area of service, one of the major considerations would be provision of a house for his family to live in. Knowing that the walls of the city were destroyed and the city was in a state of disrepair, Nehemiah wanted to plan in advance to build a new home, or to repair the governor's home in Jerusalem if one already existed.

A second area in which I believe Nehemiah demonstrated the priority of his family life is seen in 2:11–12. When Nehemiah first came to Jerusalem, he indicated that he did not conduct any official business during the daytime hours. And yet at the end of this three-day period he had a working plan to motivate the people to do the work and a strategy on how to place the people for the work. How was he able to get such a plan when he said he did not go out in the daytime? He said he went out at night.

The Hebrew word for "night" (*layil*) is the same word regardless of whether it is used in the singular or the plural. So Nehemiah could have ventured out either one night or all three of the nights. In cases where words have the same spelling in the singular as the plural, we must depend upon the context for a more definitive answer. Though Nehemiah had heard accurate reports of the physical conditions of the walls of Jerusalem while he was still in the palace at Shushan, and even though he had completed a thorough research of the situation while at the palace, he could not have had the complete picture of the enormity of the situation without seeing it for himself. And it would have taken more than one night for it all to soak in. I believe that Nehemiah went out at least two of the three nights to personally survey the condition of the walls and to devise a working strategy of how to rebuild them and to motivate the people.

What about Nehemiah's Activities During the Day?

It is during this three-day interval that I believe Nehemiah demonstrated the high priority he placed upon his family life. I believe that there were at least three things Nehemiah was doing during this time that evidence his commitment to his family life.

One of the major items on Nehemiah's list of things to do during the first three days was to get his family settled into their new home. There were boxes to unpack and things to put away into new places. Just like moving to a new home today, there are always new towel racks to put up, furniture to arrange and nothing ever seems to fit quite like it did at the previous home. Several decisions need to be made in setting up a new household. I believe that Nehemiah was there to help his family unpack and get settled into their new home. Then at least in two of the three nights he went out to make some preliminary observations of the condition of the city.

Another area of family responsibility that I believe Nehemiah gave himself to during that first three-day period is one that will be difficult to understand by those who were born and raised in the same general locality all of their life. For those of us who have known what it is to leave home, friends, and security to go off to another area of ministry, we will be able readily to identify with Nehemiah on this point.

Moving one's family to another location, even under the evident knowledge that the move is in the will of God, is a traumatic experience. The first few days are the most stress-filled and also when the enemy seems to strike the hardest at bringing discouragement to the family.

In moving the family to a new city, as Nehemiah did, there is the seemingly insurmountable work of getting settled in and the uncertainty of leaving behind all the security that was held dear. Nehemiah knew this and he set aside the work that the Lord had called him to do in Jerusalem, in order to give attention to the physical and emotional needs of his family—a higher life priority. He knew that as a husband and a father, he needed to be the one visible evidence of stability to which the other family members could look. Then at night time, after his family responsibilities had been taken care of, he left them to begin the work that the Lord had called him to do.

One last area I believe that Nehemiah gave himself to during that three-day interval had to do with the education of the children. It was the responsibility of the father to direct and oversee the education of his children.

During their younger years this responsibility was delegated to the wife; after age 12, the father played a more active role in the children's education. Although the fathers were responsible for the education of their children, they often delegated the responsibility to the local synagogue while they still maintained oversight. During the time of the captivity and the early return, Jewish fathers were concerned that their children did not know the foundations of the law that they themselves had learned in their homeland. The synagogues became centers of learning for Jewish children, teaching them the law as well as other educational courses.

While at Shushan, Nehemiah probably would have had his children enrolled at a local synagogue for their education, or at least part of it. But in moving to Jerusalem he would need to get his children reenrolled in a local synagogue so they could continue on in their education, if one was available. It was not quite that simple though. There was more than one synagogue and each one taught the law a little differently. We know for instance that at the time of Christ, there were 480 synagogues in Jerusalem,[2] each one teaching the Law with different assumptions and different emphases. It would take time for Nehemiah to get his children reenrolled in school again.

Nehemiah knew the biblical order of his life priorities, and he governed his family life and his ministry responsibilities by them. The redevelopment pastor must also keep the priority of his family in balance with the other priorities of his life and ministry or else nothing of any significance will take place. As someone has so aptly put it, "In life, the main thing is to keep the main thing the main thing." Keeping the correct balance of priorities is something which will take effort and planning in the life of the redevelopment pastor. As one pastor recently confided, "I know I need to reexamine my priorities when my wife calls my office and asks for an appointment."

What Are the Four Biblical Priorities of Life?

1. Relationship with God

The first priority for any man has to be his personal relationship with the Lord. In Matthew 6:33, we are told to "seek first his kingdom." Again, the Bible tells us that we were called into His fellowship (1 Corinthians 1:9). But what does it mean for a man to have fellowship with the Lord? It means that he not only knows the Lord Jesus Christ as his personal Lord and Savior, but that he also has a growing relationship with Him. His spiritual life is being enriched by his personal Bible study, his daily quiet time, his commitment to Scripture memorization, his daily prayer time, his fellowship with other growing Christians, and his personal testimony of God's working in his life and a desire that others know the Lord as he does. A man's relationship with the Lord is foundational; out of it flows all of his other relationships and his ministry.

2. Relationship with Family

The second biblical priority of every man is that of his relationship to his family. At this point some would substitute one's relationship to his church as second and the family as third, but the Bible places the family above the church in the order of the life priorities.

In both First Timothy 3:1–7 and Titus 1:5–9, the Scriptures set forth the character and spiritual qualifications for one desiring to become a spiritual leader in the church. In both lists of qualifications, the man's ability to rule his own household well is one of the qualifications to be a spiritual leader in the church. This would indicate that the priority of the family is higher than that of the church. A man's spiritual ministry must be demonstrated first within his family before he can be considered as a candidate for a position of spiritual leadership.

This does not mean that the pastor or spiritual leader should resign his position at the first sign of conflict within his family. If that were true, the attacks of the devil upon the family relationships of spiritual leaders would be even greater than they are now. In First Corinthians 11:18–19, the Bible tells us that one way in which God demonstrates whom He has approved as leadership in a family, or in a church, is through the process of settling conflicts. Some conflicts take longer to work through than others. It is not conflict that declares a man ineligible to be a spiritual leader; it is how he handles it in his family or in his church that will either demonstrate he is God's man for the hour, or that he is disqualified.

Jay Adams cites five reasons why a pastor must learn to rule his house well:

1. The principles and skills of management are the same where ever they may be applied.
2. If he has failed with fewer persons, how can he succeed with the increased managerial burdens occasioned by managing a whole congregation?
3. If his own home is poorly managed, this will create intolerable burdens for him that, together with the regular tasks of the pastorate, will destroy his effectiveness as a pastor.

4. If he fails as a manager in his own home, there is no way that he can become the example that so many members of the flock so desperately need to show them concretely how to manage their homes.
5. If he is allowed to assume the pastorate under such circumstances, he is being encouraged to reverse God's priorities. Instead, he must be exhorted to put first things first. He is in no shape to take on the second task until he has displayed ability in performing well at the first.[3]

3. Relationship with the Local Church

The leader's relationship to his local church is the third biblical priority of life. In Matthew 16:18, Jesus said that He was going to build His church, and He set out to do that through His people from the day of Pentecost onward, and will continue to do so until the day of the rapture. That to which the Lord Jesus Christ has committed Himself as His primary instrument of evangelism and discipleship in this world is the local church. If a man's first priority—his relationship to the Lord—is in focus, he must of necessity be committed to that which the Lord Jesus is committed to in this world, and that is the local church. One cannot be committed to the Lord Jesus and not be committed to His church. This relationship between the Lord Jesus and His church is also seen in the picture of the Lord Jesus and His bride. It is the implied intensity of affection between a man and his bride that suggests that one cannot receive the groom and be indifferent to his bride without being offensive to the groom. I believe that it is received as a personal offense to the Lord Jesus to receive Him and be indifferent to His bride, the church in its local expression.

In the New Testament, the words "church" or "churches" (*ekklesia*) are found 108 times. Of those 108 passages, 83 percent of them (90 instances) refer to a local church or to a group of local churches in a given area.

All of the spiritual gifts that are given to Christians are for the benefit of the local church (1 Corinthians 12:7).

Qualifications are given in the Scriptures for those who would be spiritual leaders of the local church (1 Timothy 3; Titus 1).

Guidelines are given for bringing members of the local church into discipline (Matthew 18:15–19).

That to which the Lord Jesus Christ is committed in this present age is the local church. And the local church today needs to be a "spiritual hospital" in a world filled with sin sickness. Primarily, the church needs to be a "labor and delivery room" where the lost can become born again and receive new life in Christ. The church needs to be a "nursery" where new Christians can be brought into a loving, caring fellowship to receive nourishment and assistance in their new-found Christian life. The church needs to be a "surgical ward" where Christians can be freed of bondage to sin and have the rottenness of sin removed from their spiritual life through the "sharp, double-edged sword" of the Word of God in the church's preaching and teaching ministries. It needs to be a "recovery room" where Christians can go to be healed after surgery or from the "diseases" of the world; a place where Christians can minister to one another and encourage and strengthen one another in the Lord Jesus Christ. And, the church also needs to be a "training ground" where "interns" can receive training in ministering to the needs and hurts of others; where Christians can get not only practical teaching, but on-the-job training, as well.

This, and much more, is the ministry to which the Lord Jesus Christ has called us to build in this world as a demonstration of His love and mercy toward lost sinners.

4. Relationship with the Lost

Fourth in the list of biblical priorities is the man's relationship with those outside the family of God. This priority must be in this place for the Christian to make an impact for Jesus Christ on the world in which he lives.

The first priority must be active in order for the fourth to take place. If I am not walking in obedience to the Lord and enjoying His presence and blessing in my life, why would I want anyone else to have what I have? The Christian's quality of life shows the attractiveness of the Lord to the lost and causes them to desire to know Him.

The second priority is also one that will demonstrate the attractiveness of the Lord Jesus Christ and the life that He offers to all who will receive Him as their personal Lord and Savior. In a time when family problems are at an all-time high, when parent-teen relationships are in constant tension, when the break-up of the family unit heads the feminist agenda, the lost of this world must see that the gospel of Jesus Christ not only affects their own eternal state, but also makes an impact upon their present life and family. For some, this priority in action will be not only what they are looking for, but also what attracts them to the Lord Jesus.

The third priority must be in place if the fourth priority is to be active also. The lost of the world need to see that the Church of our Lord Jesus Christ is not just a religious club that meets on Sunday and Wednesday. They need to *see* that the Church is a congregation of redeemed people who are committed to the Lord Jesus Christ and to one another. This will also be an attractive quality of the Christian life that will draw people to the Lord Jesus Christ.

In First Corinthians 14:24–25, Paul tells us that when an unbeliever enters the assembled church and hears the gospel being proclaimed clearly, it has an effect upon his heart. One of the first effects of the Word of God as it is preached clearly and simply is that the unbeliever feels conviction of sin. The Word of God goes deep into his heart, beyond the masks and barriers behind which no man can penetrate. But the ministry of the Word of God goes beyond conviction of sin and on to the giving of direction as to what to do. It leads the unbeliever to repentance and on to finding forgiveness and salvation in the Lord Jesus Christ. As this takes place in his heart, he becomes convinced that truly the Lord God was in that place and that he met God.

Jesus Christ has committed to us the ministry of reconciliation (2 Corinthians 5:19); He uses people to win the lost to

Himself. And when a Christian has his priorities of life in biblical order, then his life takes on an attractiveness that will be used of the Lord Jesus to draw the lost to Himself.

Working out the Four Priorities

In summary, the four priorities must be held in the order in which the Scriptures place them. One must have a personal relationship with the Lord Jesus before one can be the mate God expects. And, one of the qualifications to be a spiritual leader within the local church is the ability to lead one's family well. And, in order for the church to reach the world for Jesus, there must be an attractiveness in one's commitment to the Lord Jesus Christ and to other people. In order for the world to come to know Jesus Christ as their Lord and Savior, Christians must first live their lives with biblical priorities in order, or else the world will fail to see demonstrated any difference that Jesus Christ makes in our lives.

One's commitment to Jesus Christ can and must be seen in three areas of life:

1. One cannot profess to love the Lord Jesus with all his or her heart and at the same time hold His church to be of little or no value. The Christian who is committed to Jesus Christ as Lord will also demonstrate a commitment to a local, Bible-believing church.
2. One's commitment to Christ is seen also in the commitment to build up the body of Christ, both numerically and spiritually. When the world sees that Christians who claim to love the Lord Jesus also love one another and are committed to one another, then their testimony is powerful (John 13:34–35).
3. The Christian's commitment to Jesus Christ as Lord must be seen in the commitment to winning the world for the Lord Jesus. We cannot claim to love Him with all of our heart and at the same time not be concerned with obeying Him and winning the world to Him. Nehemiah was a man who demonstrated to all that he lived with his life priorities in their biblical order.

Before we can leave this discussion of the biblical priorities of life we have to ask some questions. What happens when one priority crowds out another? What happens when a man is so engrossed in meeting the needs of his family that he is unable to fulfill his responsibilities in his local church? Or what happens when a Christian is so involved in the activities of the local church that no time is left to reach the world for Jesus Christ?

There will always be enough time and resources for Christians to fulfill their responsibilities in each of their God-given priorities. The Lord would never lay upon us any responsibility without also giving us everything we need to fulfill that responsibility; and this includes time as one of the resources available to us.

When Priorities Clash: Two Biblical Examples

One classic example of the interweaving of life priorities occurs in John 19:26–27, when the Lord Jesus was upon the cross of Calvary. No one would dare say that the Lord Jesus was not doing the work of God in suffering and dying for the sins of the world. And yet He recognized His human responsibility He had for the future care of His earthly mother. It is generally regarded that Mary's husband Joseph was dead at this point and the responsibility for the welfare of Mary fell on the shoulders of the eldest son—in this case, Jesus. Jesus knew that His earthly brothers and sister were not believers and He wanted His mother to be taken care of spiritually as well as physically. So He entrusted John with the care of Mary and she lived with John the rest of her life. Here the Lord Jesus Christ interrupted the work of God in order to carry out family functions for which He was responsible. When priorities clash and both are in the will of God, one priority must be postponed for another to be completed.

Every Christian, especially when involved in full-time ministry, needs to learn to say "no" in the will of God. On the eve of Jesus' crucifixion, He could say in His prayer to the Father, "I have brought you glory on earth by completing the work you gave me to do" (17:4). He had not done everything, but

He had done all that the Father had given Him to do. And we must learn that we also cannot do everything, but we can, and must, do all that He has given us to do.

For the redevelopment pastor, this is a lesson that cannot be emphasized too much. If the enemy sees that he cannot keep the redevelopment pastor from responding to the call of God upon his life to come to a declining ministry, he will seek to overwhelm him with all that must be done and try to get the pastor to become out of balance in his life priorities. The devil hopes that he can get the pastor so involved in the work of the ministry that he will soon neglect his responsibilities to his family and in maintaining his relationship with the Lord Jesus.

It is possible for the pastor to become so involved in serving the Lord that he has no time to spend with the Lord; he soon "burns out" and/or loses his vision. There is always enough time and resources available for the Christian to fulfill each of life's priorities and responsibilities.

Where the Rubber Meets the Road

When the redevelopment pastor accepts a call to a declining ministry, he must take into account the needs of his family as Nehemiah did. He needs to keep the priority of his family in right perspective; how he manages his family life will either qualify him or disqualify him in the larger ministry of the Lord's service. One of the major considerations for a redevelopment pastor in coming to a declining ministry is adequate provision for his family, of which housing is vital. Here, as in most other responsibilities of the Christian life, there is a dual aspect of this point. On one hand is the fact that "my God will meet all your needs according to his glorious riches in Christ Jesus" (Philippians 4:19); on the other hand the Scriptures tell us that "if anyone does not provide for his relatives, and especially for his immediate family, he has denied the faith and is worse than an unbeliever" (1 Timothy 5:8). No matter how deep a pastor's religious convictions may be, if he has neglected his family in areas where he could have provided for them, he will be counted worse than an unbeliever and be a bad testimony for the Christian life.

Like Nehemiah, the redevelopment pastor needs to balance faith and works on this issue. Nehemiah had a financial commitment from his sending agency to meet the physical needs of his family prior to his coming to Jerusalem. In sending the redevelopment pastor to a declining ministry with the hope of turning it into a growing ministry, the sending agency should make a commitment to finance the work.

There are three means by which sending agencies seem to support new works or redevelopment works:

1. The sending agency commissions the pastor to the work but does not give him any support on which to live or work. It is expected that he will support himself with a secular job on the side.
2. The sending agency provides large subsidies to support the pastor and the work.
3. Partial support is given on which the pastor and his family can live for the first two years, and then it is tapered off with the new, or redeveloped, work picking up more and more of his salary each pay period.

It is my estimation that only the third way is best for the pastor and his family as well as for the church. If the sending agency thinks the work is important enough to begin or redevelop, they should ensure that the pastor has enough to live on modestly, but too large a subsidy can cause a new or redeveloped work to become dependent upon the subsidy and not step out on their own and take up their own responsibilities.

From the beginning, the new or redeveloped work should share in the expenses as much as they can, including the pastor's salary. In my opinion, the sending agency should recognize the limitations of the new work and give partial support as well. However, the church should know that the partial support will be tapered off after a predetermined period of time and that they will be expected to begin taking up the slack at that point, if not before.

Many times the redevelopment pastor will not have the abundance of financial resources that Nehemiah had (Nehemiah 5:14–19), so he will need to secure some commitment for his family's needs prior to assuming his role as the pastor of a declining ministry. If he does not ensure that these physical needs of his family are met, it will eventually become a hindrance to the work that the Lord has called him to accomplish in the declining ministry.

The redevelopment pastor needs to bear in mind that he has been called into a hard ministry and that the enemy will work hard at destroying his family life in order to negate his ministry. He must give attention to his family in the biblical order of priorities.

Chapter 6

Nehemiah's Leadership Style

[2:17]

Like Nehemiah, every leader has a particular style of leadership that characterizes his way of handling people and situations. How do you view the people you lead? Is their sole function to carry out the plans you have made? Or do you look to them for ideas and strategies? Are their ideas even important? Do you expect them to follow specific policies and procedures? Your perspective on the people you lead reveals your natural style of leadership.

Five Styles of Secular Leadership

In the secular world, it is generally accepted that there are five different leadership styles. These five styles of leaders as I have defined them are:

1. the *command leader* who leads from a very dictatorial position;
2. the *manipulative leader* who makes his decisions based upon the characteristics of the people he leads and then seeks to put his ideas across to them by a "hard sell" process;
3. the *consultation leader* who goes to the group whom he leads and gathers their thoughts and input prior

to making a decision;
4. the *participative leader* who allows the group to make
    the final decision based upon their participation in
    the decision-making process;
5. the *policy leader* who leads by making policies to cover
    every situation—leadership is given only when a new
    situation arises that is not covered by a previous
    policy.[1]

If we were to place these five styles of leadership on a
continuum, we would see that the leader toward the high end
of the continuum exercises complete control and his followers have very little freedom; and at the other end we would
see that the leader exercises very little control and that the
group has a great deal of freedom.

It will be helpful in our study to look with more detail into
these five styles of secular leadership before we examine
Nehemiah's leadership. For this purpose, I use the term
"organization" when applied to a Christian group to mean
either a church or a parachurch organization.

The Command Leader

In the first leadership style, the "command leader" makes
each and every decision himself. These decisions are made
without regard to the people whom he leads; they are made
in relation to a desired goal. He needs to have tightly defined
organizational policies which will cover every possible situation that could be faced in the operation of his responsibilities. He also relies heavily upon organizational flow
charts and stresses accountability to one's superiors in the
organization.

Command leadership is most often found in Christian
organizations. One of the main reasons for this is that many
churches or Christian organizations were founded by a single
man or a small group of people. And in the beginning the
leaders made all of the decisions that needed to be made. As
the organization grew, this command leadership continued.
After all, they felt, they were there from the beginning and

those who joined later had not yet "paid their dues." The longer others stay, the higher they may climb up the ladder of authority, but the command leader maintains strict control over the top of the heap.

A second reason why I feel that command leadership is so prominent in Christian circles is that Christians seem to view this type of leader in much the same way as they view Moses. Moses would go to the top of the mountain and meet with God, then come down to the people and tell them what they should do. Many Christians sincerely believe that this is truly God's method of leadership, and they dare not challenge someone who is a command leader.

Those under the authority of such a leader seldom exhibit any innovative thinking or initiative to start something; everything is left to the discretion of the one in charge. The command leader will rely heavily upon his authority and will not allow anything to happen within the organization unless he says so. He believes that his orders alone are best to achieve the goals of the organization, and he demands that the people carry out his orders to the letter.

The Manipulative Leader

In both the command and the manipulative leadership styles, decisions are made entirely by the leader without consulting the ones whom they lead. The big difference is that the command leader makes a decision on a "like it or lump it" basis, while the manipulative leader takes his followers' characteristics into consideration. This isn't as thoughtful as it sounds. He views the gifts, talents and abilities of the people solely to understand the best way to manipulate them into accepting and carrying out his decisions.

A variation of the manipulative leadership is where the leader makes his decision and then asks leading questions of key people within the organization. The people then think they had a part in the formation of the decision when in fact the leader coaxed the exact answers he wanted in order to sell his idea to them.

Manipulative leadership is also very evident in Christian

organizations, for much the same reasons as stated above for the command style. However, the manipulative leader presents his decisions with such phrases as: "I've been praying about this, and here is what I believe the Lord would have us do." No one will argue with an introduction so worded—that would be like arguing with the will of God!

The Consultative Leader

Third, there is the "consultation" style of leadership in which the leader is still the one who makes the final decisions facing the group. However, the big difference is that before he decides, he calls in key people in the organization and asks for their input. Here the leader genuinely seeks other opinions prior to forming his final decision. The consultation leader assumes that there are people within the organization who are committed to the goals and purposes of the organization, just as he is. Once he has gathered information such as he needs, then he will retreat to his office or other place to make the final decision. In consultation leadership he is still the leader, but he is not the primary source of information as to what is best for the group—the group itself is.

The Participative Leader

Next is the "participative" style of leadership in which the primary focus is not upon giving the organization direction, but upon making everyone in the group feel good, including the leader. Emotions play a big part in participative leadership. Here, the leader feels the best way to help the group feel good is to let them discuss all the options and then make the decision on their own as a consensus of opinion. He does not give leadership to the group unless he is called upon to do so. He then carries out the responsibility of the decision, but it is the group who has made it. Under participative leadership there is a "family" atmosphere that develops and often proves to be detrimental to the overall performance of the organization. The effectiveness of the group is often hampered if there is a division of opinions, or if the group's decision runs counter to the leader's opinion. In addition, if one member does not hold the same group goals or purposes as the others, the false sense of security, or "family" atmosphere, will break.

The Policy Leader

Last, there is the "policy" style of leadership that relies heavily upon the established policies and procedures of the organization. The leader of the group is more of a moderator than a true leader. Decisions are made by the group by parliamentary procedures. But the decisions' impact reaches beyond the present. As a result of the decisions made, group policies are set so that similar questions or situations that arise in the future are governed by the policies previously formulated. The leader is more of a diplomat and his job is to bring the group to a decision that satisfies the greatest number of the group. Since not every one always gets what he wants, compromise is the order of the day and decisions are made on a "give and take" basis. In policy leadership, there are no given absolutes; compromise is an accepted practice. The emphasis of policy leadership is on the system of rules and procedures rather than upon the relationships of the people within the organization or any given set of absolutes.

Another Style of Leadership

There is, however, another style of leadership, but it is one that will not be evidenced by those outside the realm of spiritual leadership. This style has three key characteristics and is based upon Matthew 20:25–28:

> Jesus called them together and said, "You know that the rulers of the Gentiles lord it over them, and their high officials exercise authority over them. Not so with you. Instead, whoever wants to become great among you must be your servant, and whoever wants to be first must be your slave—just as the Son of Man did not come to be served, but to serve, and to give his life as a ransom for many."

1. A Servant Among, Not a Ruler Over

The first of these three characteristics of biblical leadership is that the leader is to be a servant "among" the people, not a ruler "over" the people. This is opposite to the world's concept where the leader does not associate at all with those who are under his rule. In business, there are separate parking spaces, separate entrances, separate eating facilities, separate privileges and of course, the executive washroom. But not so in the biblical concept of leadership. The biblical leader does not sit in an office and issue proclamations; neither does he consider himself above the people, but he is a servant among the people seeking their best welfare.

Among God's people there is only one Head, and that is the Lord Jesus Christ Himself; all the rest of us make up what the Scriptures call His body of believers (1 Corinthians 12:12–31). On that basis we are all on the same level. However, we all have different roles and responsibilities to carry out. These roles and responsibilities are ones that the Lord has specifically given each of us to fulfill.

Scripture goes on to say that a primary task of those who have been given leadership responsibilities is to carry them out as servants of the whole body of believers. In Ephesians 4:12, Paul reminds us that those who have been given leadership gifts have the responsibility to bring the people of the church to their full potential—to train and equip them for spiritual service so that they all can have a ministry and build up the body of Christ, spiritually, numerically and organically.

Again, in Exodus 18:13–24, Moses listened to the wise counsel of his father-in-law, Jethro, and quit doing all the work *for* the people and became a servant *among* the people. As a result of Jethro's counsel, Moses did this by committing himself to pray for them and becoming the people's representative before God (18:19). Next, he committed himself to teach them the laws and statutes so that they would know how to live by practically applying the Scriptures (18:20). Last, Moses selected, trained, and delegated authority to able men who could be placed into positions of ministry.

This is the equipping ministry that Paul spoke of in Ephesians 4:11–12.

Last, in Acts 6:1–6, the apostles recognized that they had a responsibility as servants among the people to minister the Word of God to them and to pray for them. They did not try to "lord it over" the others in telling them how to solve the problem. They acted as servants among the people by giving them direction as to how they could solve the problem.

One final note before we leave this characteristic of biblical leadership. In Matthew 20:27, "servant" means one who is loyal to and committed to the interests of the one whom he serves. Jesus said that if we wanted to be the greatest, we had to serve others with all of our heart, looking out for their interests and not merely our own. Servanthood is a matter of the heart as well as a matter of performance.

It is possible to fulfill the duties of a servant without having a servant's heart. When a servant ceases to serve out of a grateful heart for all that the Lord Jesus Christ has done for him, then even though he carries on the same routine of duties, the end result will not be the same. The Lord will not be glorified and neither will His people be edified. William Barclay puts it succinctly:

> The world may assess a man's greatness by the number of people whom he controls and who are at his beck and call; or by his intellectual standing and his academic eminence; or by the number of committees of which he is a member; or by the size of his bank balance and the material possessions which he has amassed; but in the assessment of Jesus Christ these things are irrelevant. His assessment is quite simple—how many people has he helped?[2]

Biblical leadership is characterized by a willingness to be a servant among the people, not one who "lords it over them."

2. Servant Leaders Lead by Example

The second characteristic of biblical leadership is that the leader, as a servant, is to lead by his own personal example. This is why Paul could say, "Follow my example, as I follow the example of Christ" (1 Corinthians 11:1), and "Therefore I urge you to imitate me" (4:16). Paul could point people to the Lord Jesus Christ by living the example of a Christlike life before them as a servant-example.

The Scriptures indicate that an obedient Christian is a growing Christian. Five areas of one's spiritual life are essential for balanced development:

1. an intake of the Word of God (1 Peter 2:2);
2. an effective prayer life (John 15:7);
3. having fellowship with other Christians (Hebrews 10:24–25);
4. being a witness for Jesus Christ to the unsaved (Matthew 4:19);
5. becoming a responsible member of a local church (1 Corinthians 12:7).

If, therefore, the spiritual leader wants the people he serves to be men and women of the Word, he must show himself to be a man of the Word. If he wants them to be men and women of prayer, he must show himself to be a man of prayer. If he wants them to have a desire to fellowship with other Christians, he must first demonstrate the joy of having fellowship with other Christians. If he wants them to be soul-winners, he must first be a soul-winner. If he wants them to be responsible members of the church, he must first be a responsible member of the church himself. He must demonstrate before the people, not only by teaching but also by his life practices, those characteristics which he desires to effect in the lives of his people. That is the role of a servant-leader. Jesus did not come to *tell* His disciples to be servants. He took up the towel, washed their feet and *gave* them an example of what it means to have a servant's heart (John 13:2–20).

3. Heart Commitment, not Mere Behavioral Conformity

A third characteristic of the servant-leader is that he seeks a heart commitment, not a mere behavioral conformity. Matthew 20:28 reminds us that the reason Jesus Christ came was to give his life as a ransom for many. He came to die upon the cross in order that sinful men might have their sins forgiven and have eternal life through receiving Him as Lord and Savior. He became a servant in order to effect a change in our hearts that would be evidenced by a change in our behavior—a transfer from our old sin nature to our new nature in Jesus Christ. The one whom He calls to be His servant-leader is a growing Christian who, as he grows, changes the lives of those whom he serves.

The leadership in the secular world can coerce an outward change in behavior merely by the threat of the sanctions which they could impose. However, the servant-leader must seek the heart commitment of the person he serves. Mere behavioral conformity is not the goal of the New Testament spiritual leadership.

The servant-leader seeks to develop commitment first of all to the Lord Jesus Christ, then to the local body of believers, and then to service in and through that body. Behavioral change comes from outward stimuli, but heart commitment comes from a living, vital relationship with the Lord Jesus Christ.

As people see the servant-leader demonstrate his commitment to the Lord Jesus and then hear what the Scriptures say regarding commitment to Christ, they will desire to follow the Lord with a closer commitment.

Nehemiah: A Genuine Servant-Leader

Nehemiah was not one who ruled the people from his office, sending out directions of what he wanted the people to do. He worked alongside the people in the work on the wall. Because Nehemiah was accessible and visible to the people, they knew he was a caring servant among them. Someone has aptly said that people do not care how much you know until they know how much you care. The people of Jerusalem brought their problems to Nehemiah for his counsel because they knew he truly cared for them.

Second, as Nehemiah worked with the people on the wall, they saw how he reacted to criticism and ridicule from others. And they saw that he handled every situation by adhering to the Word of God for his life. Nehemiah was an example before them for all to see.

Third, Nehemiah had a goal of not only rebuilding the wall, but of seeking a heart commitment of the people to the Lord God. The wall was finished at the end of chapter six (Nehemiah 6:15–19), but throughout the next seven chapters Nehemiah led the people to a renewed dedication to the Lord and His Word.

Each of these instances will be developed further in the chapters to follow, but even a casual reading of the book of Nehemiah will reveal the example of his life as he lived openly and honestly before the people of Jerusalem.

One other item of note before we leave the subject of Nehemiah and his style of leadership: he knew when to be goal-oriented and when to be people-oriented. His leadership focus seemed to change with the need of the hour. When Nehemiah came to Jerusalem, he came with one purpose in mind: to rebuild the walls that had surrounded the city. He rallied the people to the work (2:9–20), assigned people to the different areas of responsibility and gave commendations to those who worked beyond his expectations (3:1–32). He was a goal-oriented leader. But when troubles came from the outside, as well as from the inside, Nehemiah shifted from being a goal-oriented leader to a people-oriented leader.

A spiritual leader needs to know when to shift from one focus to the other in his leadership. When the people understand that their pastor is genuinely interested in them as people, instead of just a work force to do the tasks at hand, two things will happen:

1. They will seek his help in understanding biblical applications for their personal problems.
2. They will begin to work for him, toward his God-given goals, with a greater degree of loyalty than ever before.

A pastor must learn when to press on toward the goal and when to stop and listen to his people.

Following Nehemiah's Example

The redevelopment pastor, like Nehemiah, needs to know as a spiritual leader that God has given specific guidelines regarding leadership style. It is not to be like leadership in the secular world, but like the approach the Lord Jesus spoke of in Matthew 20:25–28. He is to be a servant-leader among the people, leading them by example and moving them beyond behavioral change to heart commitment to the Lord Jesus Christ, His church and His service.

Chapter 7

The Call of God to Ministry

[1:11]

The call of God is upon everyone's life in one sense of the word. Jesus said, "You did not choose me, but I chose you and appointed you to go and bear fruit—fruit that will last. Then the Father will give you whatever you ask in my name" (John 15:16).

Every person who receives Jesus Christ as Lord and Savior is ordained to the ministry of bringing forth fruit, which is:

1. Christian character—the reproduction of the fruit of the Spirit (Galatians 5:22, 23) in the life of the believer;
2. Christian converts—the reproduction of fruit by others being saved through their ministry (Romans 1:13);
3. Christian conduct—the outward fruit of the evidences of godly character (Hebrews 12:11).

Just as the Lord Jesus calls some to be pastors and missionaries, He also calls some to be Christian business professionals, some to be Christian mothers, some to be Christian gas station attendants and some to be Christian sales representatives. No matter what vocation you enter, it is an opportunity to serve the Lord Jesus and be used of Him to win others to Him through it. No one is exempt.

However, the Lord God does issue the call of God for men to be pastors of churches and for men and women to be missionaries. It is this type of the call of God which I will discuss here: the call to full-time vocational ministry, and particularly the role of redevelopment pastor.

The Fundamental Issue of the Call of God to Ministry

One of the first considerations in understanding the role of the redevelopment pastor is making sure of the call of God upon the man's life. He must understand that he is under the call of God for his life and that he is not free to act upon his own.

The call of God upon a man's life is a basic part of the Lord God working through His people to reach the world. He still calls men to be pastors and He still calls men and women to be missionaries. The same God who called Abraham and Paul still issues the call to ministry today. And the call of God upon the life of the person still lays the responsibility upon him to carry out the gospel message, but the call is issued in such a way that the one called knows it has nothing to do with personal merit or ability.

Later in this chapter we will discuss three major reasons why every pastor or missionary needs to know the call of God upon his life for ministry. This specific call of God is such a fundamental issue that no one should dare enter the ministry without it. Why is a sense of "call" so necessary? What is meant by a "call" to the ministry?

We should first consider what a "call" is *not*. It is not mere vocational preference. It is not enough for a man to want to "repay" the Lord for His goodness by entering full-time ministry. And the desire for personal or social prestige is hardly sufficient for the demands of the ministry of the gospel.

A second thing that the "call" is not is the response of the man or woman to parents' ambitions for their child. There are instances where a pair of godly parents will earnestly desire that the Lord God call their child into the ministry and make that desire known to the child as well. The son or daughter, in turn, desiring to please both the parents and the Lord will enter the ministry on that basis rather than having received a genuine call from the Lord. On the other hand, John Thiessen points out that this may be part of a true call to the ministry:

> Samuel, the last of the judges and the first of the prophets, was dedicated to the Lord before his birth, and even before his conception (1 Samuel 1:20–28). Unquestionably Hannah's prayer and vow had much to do with Samuel's becoming the man he was. In the life story of J. Hudson Taylor we read that his parents had dedicated him to the Lord before he was born. God may call through a mother's or a father's ambition, but that alone is not enough.[1]

Finally, the decision for a man or woman to enter the ministry is not just one of default. It cannot be that other alternatives to give one's life to have been eliminated and the only one left is that of the ministry. Quite the opposite, the pastor or missionary whom God does call into His service is very often highly qualified to enter into secular vocations. The ministry of the Living Savior is not a place for losers. The pastor or missionary whom the Lord God calls into His service often feels an initial struggle between the call of God and the desire to excel at something else, often a well-paying secular job. What then is meant by a "call" to the ministry?

One must admit that there is a great deal of difficulty in defining exactly what a call of God is in clinical terms that can be examined. And yet, every man who has experienced the call of God upon his life knows exactly what it is and when it came. It is not that the person lacks the ability to do anything else, it is that he knows he could not do anything else and at the same time have a life pleasing to the Lord. And so the pastor or missionary yields his life to the call of God, not because it is the only choice, but because it is the highest choice.

How It Happened with Me

Perhaps a word of personal testimony would serve to illustrate the study of the call of God to ministry. My own personal call came on Easter evening, in April of 1970. I was stationed with the U. S. Air Force at Tan Son Nhut Air Base, just outside Saigon, Republic of Vietnam. That evening I had gone to the base chapel to spend some time alone with the Lord and to thank Him for the protection I had experienced in my tour of duty thus far. During my prayer time, I became aware of an inner thought that He had protected and saved me for a purpose—that purpose being His leading into the full-time gospel ministry.

Until that time, I looked forward to returning to the United States and going back to college. (I had previously been working on an architectural engineering degree.) I remember arguing with the Lord and telling Him all the reasons why I could not do what He wanted. It would mean starting all over in my education and those years of struggling in engineering school would be for nothing. I didn't like to speak before groups—it made me nervous. I was married now and it would be too much to try to raise a family and start all over in my education. I was straining now just trying to live a Christian testimony before the others around me and thought I was inadequate to be a leader, and on and on I went. (I did tell the Lord that if He would let me go back to the States and finish my architectural engineering degree that I would be an active member in my church and even design churches free of charge!)

After what I thought was an extended period of time of such arguing with the Lord and giving Him all the reasons why I could not be a pastor or a missionary, I finally ran out of excuses and I yielded to Him and to His call upon my life.

In the last 15 years there have been two distinct times of great discouragement in my ministry during which I have wanted to throw in the towel, and probably would have done so had it not been for the continuing reality of that day in Saigon when the Lord called me into the ministry.

Two Aspects of the Call

Though it is difficult, as I said before, to define the call of God upon one's life, and even though the call of God seems to come in circumstances unique to the individual, there are two common aspects that consistently characterize the call of God upon a man's life. The first is that the call is the initiative of the Lord God and not from man.

Practically speaking, we can say "by a call to pastoral work we mean the inner conviction that we have received a divine commission to the preaching of God's Word and such other duties as are associated with it."[2] It is this sense of a divine commission that underlies each recorded testimony concerning one's call. God Himself, in His plan and purpose for the ages, individually communicates to men what part He has for them to play. This assurance of being sent becomes the most vital part of our ministry in the times ahead.

The second characteristic which seems to be a common experience of a call to ministry is an inescapable inner awareness of God's direction for one's life and a desire to live a life pleasing to God.

I would emphasize the "desire to live a life pleasing to God." Someone has said that before God can use a man, He must fill him with His Holy Spirit. And before God can fill a man's life, He must cleanse him. And before God can cleanse him, He must first break him. This does not mean that before a man is called of God for ministry that he is perfect. It does mean that the desire of that man's heart is to live for the Lord Jesus Christ and be obedient to Him in any way that He reveals. The greatest need in the life of the pastor is not whether he has appropriate sermons, or how he fulfills his job description correctly, but rather the need to know that he has the call of God upon his life for the ministry. If the man does not have the call of God upon his life, he should not enter, nor continue, in the ministry until he is sure God has dealt with his own heart.

Along with the call of God to ministry being inescapable, it is communicated uniquely to the individual in terms of his life experience so that when it is received, the man knows that it is the voice of God to him directly, and that quality makes it inescapable to him. The Lord God knows his heart and He knows how to design just the right set of circumstances to communicate His call to the person in a unique and calculated manner.

Perhaps at this point something else should be raised regarding the call of God to ministry. It is a call of God upon the life of the individual to give himself wholeheartedly to the ministry. And in such a call to ministry it is implied that the one receiving the call will separate himself from all other vocational distractions that would interfere with God's call upon his life. He knows that acceptance of the call of God upon his life means he enters into a complete surrender of his whole being to the ministry of the Lord Jesus Christ.

I know that some will point to the fact that Paul was a tentmaker and supported himself at times in his ministry. But it must be remembered that this was a temporary situation. As soon as financial assistance was offered, he quit making tents and assumed the full-time responsibility for the preaching and teaching of the Word of God to which he had been called (Acts 18:1–4).

Last, when the call of God is issued to the man and he is aware of his call, there is the tendency to do as many of us have done. That is to argue with the Lord God and to tell Him all of the reasons why we cannot do what He wants us to do, regardless of whether or not it is the call of God to ministry or any issue that He places before us. To not respond positively to the revealed will of God places the person in a very dangerous position. It means he has assumed a superior understanding over the Lord God in two ways.

First, it says the person has a better understanding of things than the Lord God does. God brings a person to a point of decision and then desires for him to make a positive response as an act of trust in Him; but then the person considers the choice and rejects it. In doing so, he says, in effect, the desired response is not in his best interest, or that God has not considered all the factors involved.

Second, a negative response to the revealed will of God is

dangerous because it places too much emphasis upon human ability while at the same time discounting the working of the grace of God in the person's life. If the Lord God calls a person to a point of decision, He is very much aware of the person's abilities and inabilities. A study of the Scriptures will reveal that when the Lord God does call a person to ministry, it is not because of his natural abilities, but because of his weaknesses (see 2 Corinthians 12:9).

The call of God to ministry is a divinely and uniquely communicated commission of God to His service which is inescapable, and gives the recipient great joy and comfort in knowing that he is in the center of God's will for his life.

Why a Sense of Call Is Necessary

Now that we know what the call is, the next question, as we asked earlier, is why is it important to have a call of God to the ministry? There are several reasons which we could put forth, but let me point out three that I have observed personally:

1. The Demands of Ministry

The work of the ministry is too demanding and too difficult for a man to enter it without a sense of divine calling. I know of no other vocation which makes such great demands upon a person's life, his time, his emotions, his mental and spiritual abilities and his energies. There are times when the pastor has to leave an extremely happy occasion and go minister to someone in a personal crisis. He must learn how to shift emotional gears and be able to minister to the entire range of human experiences and emotions. He must deal with the old and the young, the carnal and the spiritual, the saved and the lost, the educated and the uneducated.

He must also be willing to work long hours. Sixty to 80 hours or more per week are not uncommon for the pastor of a growing church. There are numerous jobs that he must do each week, such as studying for weekly sermons, visitation, counseling, personal Bible study, continuing education, dealing with crises and ministry planning. And the motivation for getting all these jobs done the best he can must come from within. His motivation must be his own love for the Lord and gratitude for all God has done for him. No amount of monetary gain or human glory can continually motivate a man to serve as he needs to—only a call of God upon his life for ministry.

Further, he must learn the demands of dealing with the pressures of the ministry. Paul talked about these demands in the ministry to which he was called in Second Corinthians 11:28. After he listed all of the external, physical abuses he had suffered in his apostleship, he listed "my concern for all the churches" which he had started and ministered in.

A pastor of a redevelopment church may or may not have to deal with any physical abuses as Paul mentioned, but he will never escape the internal pressures of the ministry. He will grieve for his people when he sees them making wrong choices for their lives, because they did not seek the Lord in His Word and in prayer for the matter, nor did they seek the godly counsel of their pastor or the elders of the church. He will have great sorrow when he hears their feeble excuses as to why they cannot do what is right before the Lord. He will want so much for the people to know the joy of the Lord that it will pain him to see their indifference. These internal pressures of the ministry will demand a genuine call to the ministry if the pastor is to survive.

Finally, the redevelopment pastor must have a genuine call of the Lord to the ministry because of the great sense of being alone in the ministry. Most probably there will not be another man in the church who has the same vision for the work of the Lord in their church, nor the same intensity that the pastor will have. And I am not sure that it is possible for any layman to feel the same intensity for the church that the pastor feels. After all, if the church does not grow and develop as it ought to, life will go on for the people of the church. But the pastor's whole life is intertwined in that work. When it dies, he dies in his heart. And when people do not understand him or his vision and decide to leave, it is like ripping out his heart. At these times the pastor needs to fall back upon his call to the ministry and to his specific call to that particular redevelopment church.

The call to the ministry is a spiritually stretching experience. At times one can think that he is being stretched to the point of breaking. If the call is not a personal reality the pastor will cave in, because with the divine calling comes the divine enablement for the task (Romans 1:5).

2. A Sense of Urgency Needed

A second reason why the call of God to ministry is of absolute necessity is that without it there is lacking a sense of divine urgency and divine importance to the nature of the ministry. In First Corinthians 9:16, Paul speaks of this same divine urgency and importance in the ministry. "Yet when I preach the gospel, I cannot boast, for I am compelled to preach. Woe to me if I do not preach the gospel!"

Inherent in the call to the ministry is a sense of importance. It is God Himself who has called the man into ministry. And when God calls a man it is important, and that to which he has been called is important. The eternal souls of men and women lie in the balance. If the man responds to the call of God, He will use him to reach men and women, boys and girls, with the gospel and they will be saved and find eternal life in heaven forever. But if he refuses the call of God upon his life, those men and women, boys and girls will spend a Christless eternity in the lake of fire. And their blood will be upon his hands.

It is this sense of urgency which gives the importance to the call of God to the gospel ministry. The call of God to the ministry is the most important calling in the world. Any man who responds to the call of God upon his life for the ministry of the gospel must know the grave importance to which he has been called. To leave the ministry for any other position in the world, even the presidency of the United States, is a long step down in the eternal plan of the Lord Jesus Christ.

When God called Barnabas and Saul in Acts 13, it was because He had a job for them to do. When God called Isaiah in Isaiah 6, it was because He had a job for him to do; and so

it was also with Job (Job 1) and David (Psalm 139), and
Jeremiah (Jeremiah 1). And He is still calling out men to be
pastors of His church and men and women to be missionaries
of the gospel in foreign lands. Nothing is more urgent and
nothing is more important!

3. The Attacks of the Enemy

When adverse circumstances develop in the ministry, and
at some time or other they will, it is the sense of the call of
God upon a man's life and ministry that will see him through.

Anytime the devil sees a pastor having a fruitful ministry,
he will do all he can to thwart that ministry (Acts 6:1). Striking
at the leader's call is the primary focus. If he can get the pastor
to resign prematurely, Satan knows the work will fold and he
will gain the victory. It is here that the pastor needs to be
absolutely sure of the call of God to ministry upon his life.

Nehemiah's Call

In the first chapter of Nehemiah, we have the record of his
call to the ministry at Jerusalem. And, as described above, the
call originated with God and was an inescapable reality in his
life. Every genuine call has its own uniqueness, and through
the originality of personal circumstances the divine call is
mediated to the individual soul. With Nehemiah, it began one
day while he was going about his activities in the palace in
Shushan.

The Lord God began to unfold Nehemiah's unique call to
ministry by exposing him to the needs in Jerusalem (1:1–3).
In a casual conversation with Hanani, Nehemiah questioned
him regarding the condition of the Israelites and of the city
of Jerusalem. Hanani responded with some information that
had a lasting impact upon Nehemiah.

Many times Christians are confronted with needs all
around them, but when the Lord God is calling a man to a
specific ministry, it reaches beyond the stage of information
gathering to stir the heart. When Nehemiah heard of the
conditions of the wall, the city and the people, he took the
matter to the Lord in prayer. Nehemiah knew that it was a

matter of the hardness of heart that the conditions of Jerusalem were as such, and his own heart was stirred to identify himself with the people in prayer.

As Nehemiah prayed and fasted for the four-month period from Kislev to Nisan, the Lord began to bring about a change in his own heart. Sometimes that which we bring to the Lord as a prayer request, He returns to us as a responsibility for us to carry out. In fact, one cannot genuinely pray about a matter if he is unwilling to be used personally in bringing about an answer to his own prayer. Sometime during that four-month period, Nehemiah realized that he was God's man to bring about the fulfillment of the request that he himself had brought in prayer.

God called him into the ministry for which he had prayed. And once he was convinced of that call, he would be unshakable when adversity came, both from within and from without.

Chapter 8

Ministry = Faith + Works

[1:4–2:8]

Gene Getz, in his study of Nehemiah, identifies one of the foundational issues in the building of the wall of Jerusalem:

> Once Nehemiah became aware that he was God's man to go to Jerusalem and carry out the ministry about which he had been praying, he came face to face with one of the basic principles of ministry: the balance of faith and works. It is this balance of prayer and planning that sets Nehemiah apart as a man of God prepared to do the will of God. As Christians we must maintain a proper balance between divine and human factors in doing the will of God on earth. On the one hand Nehemiah prayed, seeking God's help, realizing it was impossible for him to solve the problem on his own. On the other hand, he applied himself diligently to do all he could to prepare himself for the moment God would open a door to the king's mind and heart.[1]

In all of our ministry done for the glory of the Lord Jesus Christ, we must seek to maintain the balance of what is our responsibility to do and what is the Lord's responsibility for which we must depend upon Him to do. When we become overly dependent upon our own abilities and resources, the final outcome is nothing more than a work of our own hands; the Lord Jesus will not be glorified and no eternal benefits will be derived from it. On the other hand, when we become overly dependent upon the Lord Jesus to do it all, we deny our own responsibilities in the matter and we become spiritually unusable to Him. The work of the Lord then suffers because of our own supposed "spirituality." But the glory of the Lord Jesus is seen, and the servant is fulfilled in his spirit, when a work is undertaken in dependence upon the Lord Jesus and which makes use of the gifts, talents, abilities and resources that He has entrusted to His people.

Step One: Prayer

The first step in any ministry that the Lord God calls one into is to seek the Lord in prayer for His direction and His purposes in that particular ministry. It is this foundation of prayer that will give a sense of solidarity to the ministry; and prayer must continue to undergird throughout the fulfillment of that ministry if it is to bring God glory. J. Oswald Sanders observed that "Since leadership is the ability to move and influence people, the spiritual leader will be alert to discover the most effective way of doing this. One of the most frequently quoted of Hudson Taylor's statements is his expression of conviction that 'it is possible to move men, through God, by prayer alone.' "[2]

No spiritual leader can have a fruitful ministry in motivating men and women to do the will of God unless he himself is a man of prayer. Prayer is that vital link of communication between God and man whereby His guidance and grace are appropriated for man's need. And yet, prayer is one of the first items to be neglected when a leader begins to develop a spirit of self-reliance. Every leader knows the joy of spending time with the Lord Jesus in prayer regarding some phase of the ministry and how refreshing it is to do so. And at the same time, it is one of the most difficult areas to maintain. Man is very prone to be self-sufficient. A man who wants to be a spiritual leader must know the necessity of prayer in his ministry if he is going to do any lasting work for the Lord. Yet, he must not use prayer as an escape from responsibility; he must learn that delicate balance between faith and works just as Nehemiah did.

In the Christian life, and especially so in spiritual leadership, the correlation between faith and works is that one's works grow out of his faith. As Nehemiah demonstrated, his plans grew out of his times of prayer; one's spiritual vitality comes from an effective prayer life. In Luke 18:1, Jesus gave a parable to teach this very same principle. In the introductory statement the Scriptures record, "Then Jesus told his disciples a parable to show them that they should always pray and not give up." The alternative given to prayerlessness is giving up, or being powerless. And in the matter of prayer, the spiritual leader must be disciplined in his prayer life. It is so easy for one's prayer life to slip away until the lack of spiritual power becomes so obvious to everyone.

In Nehemiah 1:11, Nehemiah ends his prayer with a request for God's help in speaking to the king in regard to what the Lord had placed on his heart. He knew that if he were to be able to go to Jerusalem to do all that the Lord had called him to do, he would have to get the permission of King Artaxerxes. In addition to the good favor of the king, Nehemiah also had in mind the timing of the request. He knew that if he was to do God's work in God's way, he had to wait for God's timing as well. So, for the king's good favor and the right timing of God, Nehemiah prayed and asked the Lord God to "Give your servant success today by granting him favor in the presence of this man."

The last two words of Nehemiah's prayer show how prayer puts obstacles in perspective. The one person on whom Nehemiah's trip depended was King Artaxerxes. But when he went to prayer, Nehemiah merely referred to him as "this man." He may have been a powerful political ruler in the world system, but Nehemiah knew that in God's eyes the king was just another man. And it was no problem at all for God to change the heart of "this man" and allow Nehemiah to go with his blessing and under his authority.

For four months Nehemiah had been in prayer regarding the burden of his heart to go to Jerusalem to rebuild the wall and to encourage the people. He had been praying for God to change the heart of the king (as in Proverbs 21:1) and for his perfect timing. Nehemiah 2:1–4, records the events surrounding the eventual answer to his prayers.

The day for which Nehemiah had been praying had come. He had been asking the Lord God for an appropriate time that he could make his request to the king. And now that time was here. One day when Nehemiah was going about his normal daily tasks, he unknowingly had a sad expression upon his face. The king noticed Nehemiah's countenance and asked him what the problem was. Evidently the king knew Nehemiah well enough to know that his facial expression was due to a burden of sorrow in his heart. This was a dangerous position for Nehemiah to be in since it was unlawful for anyone to be sad in the king's presence. It could have meant certain death for Nehemiah, but the hand of the Lord was upon him and the king did grant him mercy, even as Nehemiah had asked the Lord to do (Nehemiah 1:11).

Nehemiah knew his predicament, but his faith challenged him on to give full expression of what was upon his heart. Instead of getting angry, the king responded to Nehemiah's explanation with a desire to do something to relieve his friend Nehemiah's anxiety. The king responded with "What is it you want?" (2:4b). When Nehemiah heard the king say this, he couldn't believe what he was hearing. This is what he had prayed for and now it was beginning to take shape! So he offered up a short prayer again. But this time he probably prayed for wisdom, tact and boldness to lay his strategy out before the king.

When we pray about a matter such as this, we must not only pray for the solution of the problem, but also for the timing of God for it to take place. Inherent in every prayer request are two elements: content (what it is that we are asking the Lord to do) and timing (when we would like Him to do it). When we pray seeking the will of God, we must give Him the final authority as to the content and the timing of our request. An unanswered prayer may not mean the content was wrong; it may mean what we asked was in the will of God to do, but not at this time. Or, it may mean that God does want to intervene at this time, but what we asked for was not what He was wanting to do. Having a bag of gold in hand would be a great experience, but not while you are treading water several miles from the shore. Timing is an integral part of our praying.

Nehemiah's whole work for the Lord God in Jerusalem was an outgrowth of his personal prayer life. It was while Nehemiah was praying about the conditions at Jerusalem that the Lord called him to do the task. And it was in answer to a short prayer that the king granted his request for materials and his support in returning to Jerusalem. It was in answer to prayer that Nehemiah was able to devise a strategy for the rebuilding of the wall once he returned to Jerusalem. It was in answer to prayer that he was able to settle disputes between the people of Jerusalem. Everything that Nehemiah did, both in rebuilding the wall and in reestablishing God's testimony among the people and in encouraging them, came about as an answer to prayer. To Nehemiah, prayer was a vital part of his life and it was out of his prayer life that his ministry developed.

Like Nehemiah, the redevelopment pastor must be a man of prayer and let the Lord Jesus form his ministry out of his prayer life. He needs to act like a soldier reporting to his commander for orders for the day. The redevelopment pastor must be one who seeks the Lord for the direction of his life and also for his ministry. Ministry that is not developed out of one's prayer life is in danger of becoming a work of self-effort.

Step Two: A Plan

Step number two in ministry is developing a strategy out of the times of seeking the Lord in prayer. It is during these times of genuine, earnest prayer that God gives direction for His work. We will consider Nehemiah's strategy later in this chapter in more detail, but it should be noted here that it was

out of Nehemiah's times of prayer that he developed the plan
of how to get to Jerusalem and what he would need once he
arrived. It was also out of a time of prayer after he had
surveyed the conditions of the wall personally and prayed
over them that he developed his plan of how to motivate the
people to repair the walls and how each person would play a
part in working on a particular section of the wall. Human
reasoning could have never accomplished the work for God
that Nehemiah did.

It must be remembered that he was not a contractor, nor did
he have construction experience; he was a man available to be
used of God, with a plan that was developed after spending
ample time in prayer. Planning without first seeking the Lord
earnestly in prayer only leads to disaster. On the other hand,
prayer without planning leads to a Christian becoming ir-
responsible in those duties that the Lord God places upon His
people in the carrying out of His plan for the ages.

There are numerous instances in the Scriptures where the
Lord Jesus requires action balanced with our faith. In Matthew 4:19, Jesus said "Come, follow me . . . and I will make
you fishers of men." If I follow him (an exercise of faith) then
I will become a fisher of men (a required action). In Acts 1:8,
Jesus again said, "You will be my witnesses." A witness is one
who merely tells what he has seen or heard. But if I am not
living for the Lord Jesus, I will not have anything to tell others
about. Planning without prayer is just as much an exercise of
disobedience as prayer without planning.

In Second Corinthians 5:18, the Bible tells us "All this is
from God, who reconciled us to himself through Christ and
gave us the ministry of reconciliation." The fact that the Lord
Jesus has committed this ministry to us is seen in Acts 8, 9
and 10. In Acts 8:26–40, we read that the Lord God had been
working in the heart of an Ethiopian man, creating a hunger
in him for things of the Word of God and a humble spirit
that would receive instruction. But the Lord God would not
lead this man to Himself. The ministry of reconciliation had
been committed to believers and He sent for a man—Philip—
to come lead the Ethiopian man to Himself and baptize him.

In Acts 9:1–19, we read of the conversion of Saul of Tarsus. The Lord Jesus revealed Himself to Saul while he was on his way to Damascus and blinded him so that he had to be led away by another. The Lord could have also made him receive his sight again and be healed, spiritually and physically, but He did not do it. He sent for a man—Ananias—to come and do it for Him. He has committed to us the ministry of reconciliation.

In Acts 10, we see the conversion of Cornelius, his relatives and his neighbors. The Lord had been working in Cornelius' heart and had brought him to the point of salvation, but the Lord would not do it Himself. He had Cornelius send for a man—Peter—who led them all to Jesus Christ as Lord and Savior, because He has committed to us the ministry of reconciliation.

The redevelopment pastor must be a man of prayer and also a man of planning and action. And he must know the balance of the two in order to have an effective ministry. Gene Getz comments:

> Our relying on prayer alone is never God's way of achieving His goals on earth. Merely trusting Him as the Sovereign of the universe is a superficial approach theologically. He is indeed sovereign, but He has placed upon all of us significant human responsibility. It is sometimes difficult to balance these two concepts pragmatically, but it is absolutely essential in order to be effective in our ministry for the Lord.[3]

Nehemiah's Strategy

Nehemiah was so sure that the Lord God was indeed going to honor his prayers that as he prayed, he also made plans and developed a strategy for rebuilding the walls of Jerusalem:

1. He Assessed the Problem

Nehemiah had a knowledge of the general condition of the

city and of the people (Nehemiah 2:3) even though he had not been there. Four months had passed since Nehemiah had first heard of the conditions of the city and of God's people. It is not recorded what Nehemiah did during this interval, but from the events that followed, we can guess what he was doing. When the king finally asked Nehemiah what he wanted him to do, Nehemiah had it all worked out. During those four months, Nehemiah was working and praying through a strategy to do the work that the Lord had called him to do.

2. He Estimated the Needed Resources

A second aspect of Nehemiah's strategy that he developed in Susa, after spending time in prayer, is that he also knew, generally, what resources he would need to get the job done (2:5–8) and where to get them. Nehemiah had requested enough timber to build up the gates of the city and of the temple as well as enough timber to build himself a home in which to live while in Jerusalem. He had found out about the sycamore forest in the low plains, which had been the property of King David (1 Chronicles 27:28, 31 and Nehemiah 2:8). He not only knew where it was, he knew by name the one who was in charge of it. Nehemiah had completed his homework in researching what materials would be needed and where he could get them, and, who would pay for them.

3. He Estimated the Time Needed

A third aspect of Nehemiah's strategy was that he had also worked out a timetable estimating how long it would take him to get the job done (Nehemiah 2:6 and 13:6). King Artaxerxes had grown very fond of Nehemiah and trusted him to be a man of his word. In the king's reply to Nehemiah regarding the time element involved came the answer to prayer that Nehemiah had been seeking. The king had granted his request to return to Jerusalem. The only issue to be worked out now was how long Nehemiah was to be gone. Nehemiah had become such an asset to the palace staff that the king did not want to let Nehemiah go forever.

In the king's reply to Nehemiah, he once again let

Nehemiah know how much he trusted him. The king did not set a timetable or fix a time for Nehemiah to return to the palace. He left the final decision to Nehemiah, and that was an example of how much the king trusted Nehemiah's judgment. And Nehemiah did not disappoint the king. He had sought counsel, studied the situation from the palace and had arrived at a workable timetable as to how long it would take him to complete the task. No detail was left unnoticed—that was the way Nehemiah did things.

4. He Assessed the Obstacles

Last, Nehemiah was also aware of some of the obstacles that would hinder his getting the job accomplished (2:10). Israel still had several enemies and they would not be too anxious for Nehemiah to come and restore Jerusalem and encourage the people. Cyril J. Barber states:

> He was also cognizant of the obstacles that might prevent the successful completion of his assignment. He knew that before he could begin rebuilding the city, he must have safe passage through the different provinces. He was aware of the dislike of the different satraps for the Jews, and knew that they and their subordinate officials might interrupt his journey and hinder his work unless he had authoritative credentials to present to them. Only the king's seal would do.[4]

Because Nehemiah had thoroughly studied out the situation in Jerusalem and the obstacles of doing the work, he was able to make plans as to how to react when the potential obstacles came into reality. In doing so, he was able to take away one of the greatest weapons of the enemy, that of the element of surprise. Just because a man knows the call of God upon his life does not mean that he will never know adversity in his ministry—just the opposite! The greater the ministry, the greater the obstacles and greater the adversity. The redevelopment pastor above all else must know this and make plans accordingly.

Nehemiah had completed his homework as well and had sought the Lord God in prayer. He had learned, and had demonstrated, the delicate balance in the Christian life and ministry of faith and works; of prayer and planning.

Chapter 9

The Value of Personal Observation

[2:12–16]

After Nehemiah's requests were granted to him by King Artaxerxes, he was ready to leave for Jerusalem. We do not know how long it was before he was ready to make the two-month journey from Shushan to Jerusalem, but we do know that his success before the king did not cause him to be filled with pride.

"From a human point of view Nehemiah was a man who made things happen," Gene Getz comments. "But unlike so many today, when things happened he knew it was not only his human ingenuity and his hard work that caused it but also God's blessing upon him."[1]

Nehemiah knew that any success he might have had was a direct result of his walk with the Lord and the grace of God upon his life to do the will of God. Others might have looked at him and thought he was "a mover and a shaker," but Nehemiah knew it was the blessing of God. And all of the hard work a person can do in planning out the best of strategy, studying all the details, setting forth various options and employing human psychology cannot produce what the blessing of God can upon a man who is open to do the will of God.

Not only did the king grant Nehemiah his requests, but he gave him even more than Nehemiah had asked for. In

Nehemiah 2:9, Nehemiah records that "The king had also sent army officers and cavalry with me." Even though Nehemiah did not ask for the escort, I believe the king sent it for at least two major reasons. Artaxerxes was a knowledgeable man and he knew of the dangerous trip between Shushan and Jerusalem. He was expecting Nehemiah to make the trip back to Shushan at the end of the time agreed upon. But he could not come back if he were to be attacked and killed on the way there. The king was protecting his trusted servant, Nehemiah. Second, to send an escort would signal to all how much the king honored Nehemiah. Nehemiah had been a high official of the palace and now he was to be a governor of Jerusalem. The king wanted everyone to know Nehemiah was a valued ambassador and a king's escort signified this.

Nehemiah's life is a vivid testimony to all of us who would enter the ministry of our Lord Jesus Christ. It was not his personality, ingenuity or ability to plan things out that made him the success he was; it was his personal walk with the Lord. Upon his arrival in Jerusalem Nehemiah did not first of all jump into the work which he came to do. In chapter five we discussed the four priorities of a man in full-time Christian service and how the four interrelate. We came to the conclusion that Nehemiah took those first three days to meet the physical, emotional, educational and spiritual needs of his family before jumping into the work the Lord had called him to do.

No Greeting Party Here!

One thing is noticeably absent from Nehemiah's arrival in Jerusalem. Picture this scene in your mind. An envoy arrives from the palace of the king that contains the king's cupbearer (a highly esteemed position) and the king's army, and a number of horsemen, but no one came out to greet them as would be expected upon the arrival of such high governmental officials. Matthew Henry observed that "it does not appear that any of the great men of the city waited on him to congratulate him on his arrival, but he remained unknown. The king sent horsemen to attend him, but the Jews sent none to meet him."[2] This absence of a greeting party tells us something about the condition of the people at Jerusalem.

It could be that they were angry at the king and did not care if he sent them a new governor or not. In the book of Ezra, it is recorded that the work on the temple was periodically stopped because reports went to the king that Israel was a rebellious people. The people had not always enjoyed a good working relationship with the king. So it is not unusual to think that they were not emotionally moved when a new governor came to rule over them.

Another possibility is that the people were too embarrassed to go out and meet him. They were used to living in the rubble and were intimidated to think of meeting one who had come from the king's palace to such a mess as that.

Discouragement, too, could have kept the people from coming out to meet Nehemiah and the king's envoy. They had been living in such discouraging surroundings and thinking that nothing could ever change. They might have given up hope and were at an all-time low in their lives.

Whatever the reason, no one came out to meet Nehemiah as he came into the city.

This should be a note of consideration for the redevelopment pastor as he comes to take up his new ministry to which the Lord has called him. Don't expect a big welcoming party nor the cheers of those to whom you have come to build up and encourage. You must remember that just as there are reasons why a church grows, there are also reasons why a church declines. And it is evident that some of those reasons are present. Remember also that changing those conditions will not be easy. Most likely other pastors have come here before with great plans and a lot of enthusiasm, and they soon left after feeling defeated. The people who stay in the declining church are left to hold things together, when pastor after pastor comes with his plans and zeal then leaves in a year or so.

The redevelopment pastor, who needs the cheers of the people to motivate his ministry rather than reliance upon the call of the Lord to ministry, will also be packing his bags in a year or so.

Take a Look for Yourself

When Nehemiah first arrived in Jerusalem he did not call for a meeting with the leaders of the city, nor did he take a survey of the people. In fact, he did not consult with anyone. He merely went out each evening and made a personal inspection. Nehemiah had heard the reports from the brethren while he had been in Shushan in the palace, but he needed to observe personally the conditions of the city and of the people and to get those conditions firmly embedded into his mind.

The redevelopment pastor, like Nehemiah, needs to make a personal observation of the ruins before he can fully assess the situation. He cannot consult the people nor the leaders of the church. He can only observe and pray for wisdom from the Lord Jesus. A word of caution at this point—the redevelopment pastor needs to be careful about making too many changes too quickly after his coming. If the pastor is one step ahead of his people, they will recognize him as their leader. But if he is too far ahead of them they may think he is the enemy and begin to shoot at him. Being one step ahead of the people makes a pastor a leader; being 10 steps ahead makes him a martyr.

There are several reasons why the redevelopment pastor needs to survey the situation personally as did Nehemiah with the walls of Jerusalem.

The first reason for a personal observation is that people often overlook the "rubble" when it becomes familiar. They do not even see it. Every pastor needs to take a clipboard the first week of his new pastorate and make a personal inspection. He needs to make note of those things in the facility that need to be corrected—unfinished tasks, areas in need of repair, objects and walls that need paint. If a pastor has not done this inspection within the first three weeks of his new pastorate, he needs to get someone who does not come to his church to make the observations for him. When visitors come to our churches, they see all these areas that need attention; but we have a tendency to overlook them because we have become used to seeing them and have blocked them out of our minds.

Nehemiah knew this tendency of the human nature and as soon as he was able to dispatch his family responsibilities, he set out to personally survey the walls. Such a report would be impossible to get from anyone who lived in Jerusalem because they would be unable to look upon the familiar with an objective eye.

The second reason for the redevelopment pastor to do as Nehemiah did and make a personal observation of the facilities soon after his arrival is that those who lived in Jerusalem were a discouraged people and had lost their vision; they could not give an accurate, objective evaluation of their situation. People who live in the "rubble" of a declining ministry, such as fallen Jerusalem, become accustomed to their situation and in the process lose their vision. These people had left their homes in the various places of their captivity in Persia to go back to Jerusalem, with hopes of one day regaining the glory in Jerusalem that once was there. But through a series of discouraging events, they lost their vision and needed someone such as Nehemiah to come "stir their fires." As a man with a vision from God concerning Jerusalem, Nehemiah could not enlist the help of those who had lost their vision to help him survey the wall; he had to do it personally. Nehemiah also knew that he had not come to Jerusalem at the invitation of the people but in response to the call of God. He needed to seek the Lord as to what He thought of the matter and how He wanted it changed. People with a lost vision are not capable of doing what needs to be done.

Third, very often those who live in the "rubble" of a declining ministry have developed a negative spirit and can only say why their situation will never change. After all, from their point of view, what difference could Nehemiah make? When Zerubbabel left to return to Jerusalem, he had high hopes of rebuilding the wall and the city, but he failed. Then, years later, Ezra returned to Jerusalem with the same aspirations and the city was still in a state of sad disrepair. If Nehemiah would have came back to Jerusalem and shared his burden with the people then, they would only tell him that others had tried and failed and that nothing would ever change.

There is inherent in the heart of a man of vision a spirit of optimism and hope. "Vision includes optimism and hope. No pessimist ever became a great leader. The pessimist sees a difficulty in every opportunity; the optimist sees an opportunity in every difficulty."[3] He sees beyond what is, to what will be. He sees opportunity in difficulty. But he also knows that if he surrounds himself with those who have lost their vision that their negative attitudes will soon affect his own. The less contact that he has with people who have no vision, the more he will be able to carry out that which the Lord God has placed in his heart to do.

Nehemiah had heard in his earlier conversation (1:3) that the people were discouraged and now he had seen for himself, not only the condition of the wall, but the condition of the people. They may not have paid much attention to him, but he observed them and knew their discouraged state.

It takes a man of vision to see beyond what *is* to see what *can be*. "Christian leadership demands vision," declares Ted Engstrom. "The Christian leader must have both foresight and insight. When he does, he will be able to envision the end result of the policies or methods he advocates. The great missionary pioneers were without exception men of vision: they had the capacity to look beyond the present."[4] Nehemiah was such a man.

Look and Pray

When observing the situation of a declining ministry, the redevelopment pastor must bathe his observations in prayer. Nehemiah was a man of prayer and he must have prayed earnestly as he was viewing the ruins of the walls.

One of the reasons I believe he must have prayed while he was surveying the wall has to do with his occupation. Nehemiah was a cupbearer, a political servant/advisor who served in the palace court. He was not a contractor, nor is it recorded that he had any type of construction experience. As he surveyed the wall he must have prayed for wisdom and guidance as to how to rebuild it. He had to develop a plan of attack as to how to clear away the rubble, how to save what materials could be saved, what new materials would be needed, and where to place the workers on the project. He observed the details of the work to be done and had the wall completed step by step in his mind while everyone else merely saw the rubble.

Another reason why I believe Nehemiah must have prayed as he observed the conditions of the wall has to do with the effect from the continual focus of one's attention. Whatever we place as the focus of our mind affects our overall attitude. Nehemiah could not have focused his mind on the broken down ruins of the walls of Jerusalem without himself becoming discouraged just as the others had become. To keep that from happening, he had to have a God-ward focus in prayer as he viewed the conditions of the walls, in order to keep from sinking into despair.

Nehemiah's Example of Observing and Praying

Nehemiah knew that in order to develop a working strategy for the rebuilding of the walls of Jerusalem, he must personally inspect the walls and bathe his observations in prayer. And the redevelopment pastor must observe and record in writing everything that he sees that needs to be changed in the first few weeks of his new ministry. Otherwise, he also will not be able to see them, and they will continue to be obstacles to the growth of the church.

Chapter 10

Motivating Others in the Work

[2:17–3:32]

At this point in his life, Nehemiah had come to a crossroad. For four months he had prayed earnestly regarding the news he had received concerning the walls of Jerusalem and the condition of God's people. He had prayed for God's favor and for God's timing in bringing the matter before the king whom he served in the palace. Also during the four months, Nehemiah had sought the Lord in the development of a plan to get the work done once he was sent to Jerusalem. The Lord God had opened the door of opportunity for Nehemiah to voice his burden to the king and the king released him to return to Jerusalem and accomplish the work that the Lord had placed on his heart.

Nehemiah had spent approximately two months traveling from Shushan to Jerusalem, mulling over his plans all along the way. Once he was in Jerusalem, he settled his family into their new home and went out during the evening hours to make a personal observation of the condition of the walls. During those first three days, he was also able to get a feel for the condition of the people whom he had come to lead. Further, he had developed a strategy to implement his plan. It is one thing to have a plan to accomplish a goal, but it is another thing to motivate a group of people to help you accomplish your goal, especially when the people are used to living in rubble and are a very discouraged group.

Even though Nehemiah was the officially appointed governor, and could have ordered the people to do the work, he knew that was not the way to get the job done. He had to rouse the people and encourage them to help him accomplish the task that the Lord God had called him to do. He had to stir them to action, not because they had to obey his orders, but because they sensed God's calling upon his life and wanted to help Nehemiah in his work. Nehemiah was now ready to demonstrate his leadership by motivating the people to do the work that the Lord had called him to Jerusalem to do.

What Is Motivation?

When we speak of motivation, we usually mean one of two types: self-motivation or the motivation of others. Self-motivation is the inner drive that makes a person do the things he or she does. Motivation of others is the ability to get them to go along with someone else's plans, whether personal or third-party plans. Nehemiah was not only self-motivated but could also motivate others to do the impossible.

Others before him had tried to rebuild the city and reestablish God's testimony among the people, but they could not. Nehemiah could, and did, because he knew how to motivate the people and because he was on a mission sent by the Lord God. Kenneth O. Gangel, quoting Dr. Mungo Miller, president of Affiliated Psychological Services, identifies six general principles of motivation:

1. Motivation is psychological, not logical. It is primarily an emotional process.
2. Motivation is fundamentally an unconscious process. The behavior we see in ourselves and others may appear to be illogical, but somehow, inside the individual, what he is doing makes sense to him.
3. Motivation is an individual matter. The key to a person's behavior lies within himself.

4. Not only do motivating needs differ from person to person, but in any individual, they vary from time to time.

5. Motivation is inevitably a social process. We must depend on others for satisfaction of many of our needs.

6. In the vast majority of our daily actions, we are guarded by habits established by motivational processes that were active many years earlier.[1]

Nehemiah assembled the people and explained his purpose in coming and sought to motivate them to assist him in his efforts. Until then he had not even told the local Jewish officials of his intentions. Not much is known about who these people were or who had appointed them. Nor is it known why they did not come out to meet him as he rode into Jerusalem with the king's envoy. But the fact that Nehemiah addressed them as the rulers shows that they were important people in Jerusalem.

As Nehemiah stood before the people, he must have thought that his big moment had finally arrived. He was going to point out the problem and give his solution. (A problem defined is a problem half solved, but the second half of the problem, that of motivating the people, was a big one.)

After a four-month period of prayer and planning, a two-month trip to get there, and a three-day period of personal observation, Nehemiah was finally ready, in the timing of God, to reveal his heart to the people. But he had to be very tactful in his presentation so that the people did not feel slighted or condemned for their condition and resent him as an outsider. The speech he delivered is recorded in an abbreviated form and gives only the main points of his outline and the response of the people.

There is something noticeably absent from Nehemiah's speech before the people. He told them what needed to be done, why it needed to be done, how the Lord God had worked in his heart, and how the king had given his support with material provision and his authority to do the job. The one thing that Nehemiah did not tell them was how he was going to get the job done. He did not tell them of his ability to lead and motivate people. He did not tell them of his previous successes in the palace at Shushan. He did not point out any of the methods or principles of leadership with which he was well acquainted. He did not tell them how he would lead them in the work. He merely led them.

Here is an important lesson for the redevelopment pastor to learn when he begins his new ministry at a declining church. Many times people in a declining church will want to put their trust in the pastor and in his abilities to turn their church into the growing church it may have been previously. But the pastor needs to point them to the Lord Jesus Christ, to the needs of the ministry and to how he senses the hand of God upon his life. He should never tell them of his leadership prowess or abilities, nor of his vast knowledge of church growth and administration. He should never tell them of his skills, methods or principles. He should just lead and quietly introduce projects, programs and ministries that employ those principles in the church.

Three Outstanding Characteristics of Nehemiah's Challenge

1. Identification

In Nehemiah 2:17–18, Nehemiah first identified himself with the people in the situation as one of them rather than as an outsider coming in to tell them what to do. In 2:17 he said to them, "You see the trouble *we* are in: Jerusalem lies in ruins, and its gates have been burned with fire. Come, let *us* rebuild the wall of Jerusalem, and *we* will no longer be in disgrace" (italics mine). Nehemiah identified himself with them not only in the cause of the problem but also in the solution to the problem. Furthermore, he identified himself with them in the motivation for rebuilding the wall.

Nehemiah wanted the people to know he was one of them. He was the governmentally appointed leader over them, but more importantly, he was a man sent by the Lord God to work among them for the glory of God and for their ultimate benefit.

2. No Condemnation

A second characteristic regarding Nehemiah's stirring speech to the Jews in Jerusalem was that he forced them to see again the disrepair that they were in without condemning them for it. He could have "raked them over the coals" for allowing such a condition to exist in Jerusalem. Or, he could have sought to shame them into action. But he knew that would have been short-lived.

Such actions as these never encourage or motivate people. "When you cast blame and criticism," Chuck Swindoll says, "you squelch motivation. When you identify with the problem, you encourage motivation."[2] Too often the road that spiritual leaders take is that of condemning the people for their situation as if it is a result of their own actions. Rather than helping a declining ministry, the leader actually digs the hole of despair deeper and makes it even harder to turn the declining ministry around.

Nehemiah was positive and honest in his evaluation of the situation before the people. But he did not cast blame or ridicule upon them for allowing the situation to exist or to continue.

3. Education

Third, Nehemiah spoke of their situation as a reproach against the testimony of God, not against them. The people had learned how to live with the situation because they merely thought of it as a reproach against themselves, but they needed to see that it was not against them but against God.

As God's people align themselves with Him, the unbelieving world looks upon them and forms an opinion of what God is like by the way He is represented. Jerusalem was known as the city where the temple was located, the City of God; and when it was in a broken down situation, it reflected to the unbelieving world that the Lord God was powerless and that His people really did not care about Him.

Nehemiah was able to force the Jews to see that the condition of the walls was not merely a blot against them, but a reproach against one much higher—the testimony of the Lord God.

It has been said that there are three ways a man can destroy his life. The first way is to be lazy and do nothing. The second way is to give yourself to the wrong goals in life, work hard, and then find out your mistake at the end of your life. The third way is to give yourself to many things and never really do anything. None of these statements applies to Nehemiah— he was a mover of men. He knew what the Lord God had called him to do and he set out with a single-mindedness to do it. He could motivate others because he himself was motivated in the task.

To say that Nehemiah motivated the people of Jerusalem is not quite correct. Everybody is motivated to do what they really want to do. The real challenge of the leader is to get the people all motivated toward the goals and objectives that the Lord has placed in his heart to do.

Two Reward Systems

People are motivated by two systems of rewards:

> *Extrinsic rewards* are those that appeal to our materialistic desires. Examples of extrinsic rewards would be salary increases, bonuses, job rewards, status incentives and all other rewards that come from the outside.
>
> *Intrinsic rewards* are those that come from within ourselves. Some examples of intrinsic rewards would be the joy of achieving a goal or completing a task, satisfaction in a job well done or pride in the ability to work out a difficult problem and make the job run smoothly.

"Nehemiah did not promise any material incentives when he addressed the Jerusalem officials. He didn't offer prizes to the fastest-working families or a week at the Dead Sea for the group doing the most attractive work," Swindoll says. "Being led by God, Nehemiah was able to appeal to their intrinsic zeal."[3] People who must be constantly motivated extrinsically will tend to be carnally minded and their inner motivation is basically, "What's in it for me?"

Only those who have the maturity to be motivated intrinsically will ever be able to do a great work for the Lord Jesus Christ. This does not mean that people who are in positions of spiritual leadership should not give recognition or other expressions of gratitude to those who are under their ministry; not at all. The pastor should indeed let his people know he is genuinely grateful for their support in the ministry. However, extrinsic rewards cannot be the basic motivation for service in the ministry of the Lord Jesus Christ, either in the lives of the pastor or in the people.

The reason Nehemiah was able to appeal to their intrinsic zeal was because the people sensed he was genuinely concerned for their welfare. After all, they could see that he gave up a good palace position to come to Jerusalem to live with them among the rubble; that had to count for something in their eyes. Every spiritual leader knows that his success as a motivator will be directly proportionate to the perception of the people that he is genuinely concerned for them. If he is perceived as only being interested in them as a means to an end, or in building his own reputation by turning a declining ministry into a growing one, he will not succeed. They may follow him for a short time, but they will exit soon with a feeling of being used.

At this point, Nehemiah's motivation level was high, but let's remember that the Lord had been working in his heart concerning this goal for at least six months (four months in the palace and two months to make the trip). Nehemiah was a motivated man, and now he wanted to motivate the people for the same goals that he had come to accomplish.

A Leader's Motivation: Two Important Points

1. There is a principle stated in Second Corinthians 1:3–4 that says God first works his message *in* a man before he works that message *through* the man to others. When God uses a man to motivate others, He

first motivates the man and then motivates others
through him.

2. Enthusiasm is contagious—it is something that is
caught, not *taught*. Enthusiasm for a job or a goal is
transmitted not merely by a message about the job's
importance, but from one life to another when en-
thusiastic pursuit of the goal is seen.

Nehemiah was able to motivate the people because he had
been motivated for the job at least six months prior, and
because the people saw the enthusiasm with which he
described how the Lord God had led in his life thus far, and
his enthusiasm for the job before them.

Accomplishing the Impossible

Often those who are involved in a declining ministry have
not only lost their vision for the future, but they have
developed a survival mentality. They have given up on trying
to grow and are now fighting to survive.

Like Nehemiah, the redevelopment pastor must replace
the survival mentality held by those in the declining ministry
with a sense of hope and a glimpse of the vision that the Lord
God has given to him for their church. "Nehemiah's handling
of the situation in Jerusalem illustrates for us the essence of
good motivation," Cyril Barber notes. "The significance of
what he accomplished may be seen from the fact that for
ninety years the people had been saying, 'It can't be done!'
Now they are united and eager to begin the work of rebuilding the defenses of their city."[4]

It has been my experience that it takes about 18 to 24
months of ministry in a declining church before the people
can begin to have this change in their perspective. They must
see things that the pastor does, often without any help from
the church, that produces growth. After they see that growth
can happen, then they will begin to join in and actively
support growth activities. The redevelopment pastor must
know that a survival mentality did not come about overnight
and it will not leave overnight. Three years of ministry is not

uncommon in order to change the people's thinking toward growth.

For years the people in Jerusalem had told themselves that things would never be any different, that it was useless to think they would ever regain any measure of accomplishment. They were a defeated people and their surrounding enemies had done all they could to reinforce the people's defeated attitude. When Nehemiah stood before them, his testimony of how he knew the will of God in his coming was the main part of his message.

No congregation will ever follow any man in a ministry if they do not sense the call of God upon his life and hear his testimony to that effect. People in a declining ministry find it very hard to place their trust in the Lord to rebuild their church; they need to hear and see a man who knows God's calling upon his life and to sense his leadership.

When Nehemiah stood before the people, he told them of two ways in which the Lord God had demonstrated His will for Nehemiah in his coming to Jerusalem in order to rebuild the walls.

Testimony of His Own Life

First, he spoke of how the Lord had prepared him and brought him to Jerusalem. Nehemiah knew better than to try to take any of the credit for what had happened thus far. He knew that anyone who wants to be a leader of God's people must be a man of God and never promote himself personally. That is a sure sign that he is headed for defeat and is disqualified as a spiritual leader. In fact, every man who is a successful spiritual leader will be able to relate an experience in his life where God made him painfully aware of his own shortcomings and the uselessness of self-effort. It is a record of Scripture and the experience of spiritual leaders that before God uses a man, He first crushes a man and brings him to the end of himself, so that he will know the result of self-reliance and self-promotion.

To give a personal, public testimony of what the Lord Jesus Christ has done in your life is always projected in at least three different directions:

1. It is projected upward in that it gives glory to the Lord God for His working in your life. This is the "sacrifice of praise—the fruit of lips that confess his name" (Hebrews 13:15).
2. It is projected outward toward people. Hebrews 11:6 says, "And without faith it is impossible to please God, because anyone who comes to him must believe that he exists and that he rewards those who earnestly seek him." The world is not looking to see what we do for the Lord, but what He does for us. And we can tell them that He truly "rewards those who earnestly seek him."
3. It is projected inward to the heart of the one giving the testimony. One's own heart is encouraged and strengthened again as he recalls the blessing of God upon his life. This was the experience of Nehemiah as he spoke of how God had moved in his life in bringing him to Jerusalem.

"By pointing them away from their fears to the Lord he fixes their minds on what God is doing for them," Barber says. "This reassurance is of great encouragement to the Jews. They realize afresh that God is on their side. Their enthusiasm is ignited."[5] Nothing is more of an encouragement to trust the Lord for greater things than knowing that He is already at work and that He has provided for them in visible ways.

Testimony of Provision

The second word of testimony that Nehemiah gave to the people concerned how the Lord had provided the building materials through the king and how he had come under the authority of the king. He probably told them how he had prayed for four months and how the Lord God opened up the opportunity to speak to the king. He probably also told them of his conversation with the king and how authority was given to come to Jerusalem and do all that the Lord God had put upon his heart. He probably reminded them of the king's escort which came with him to Jerusalem. He probably showed them the letters that the king had given to him authorizing materials to be procured from the king's forest to rebuild the wall and build his own house. By telling the people of all that the Lord had already done, he ignited their enthusiasm for the work. They could sense a genuine call of God upon Nehemiah's life and they were encouraged in their hearts.

What more could the people say now? The Lord God had sent Nehemiah to Jerusalem to lead them in the rebuilding of the walls and to establish once again the testimony of God among them; and He had also worked through the heart of the king to provide for all the building materials that they would need to finish the task. At some point in Nehemiah's speech, the hearts of the people turned from defeat to hope. He had sparked them by his testimony of God's hand upon his life to a renewed vision that the wall and the city could be rebuilt and the work of the Lord could be re-established under Nehemiah's leadership.

Everyone responded just as Nehemiah had prayed that they would (Nehemiah 2:18); the people started immediately to work on the wall. This was the actual beginning of what he had come to Jerusalem to do. All of his planning, all of his prayers, all of his waiting was beginning to pay off now that the people were stirred out of their lethargy and into action. With such a quick response of the people to Nehemiah's challenge, it was a wise move for him to have had his plan in hand when the people were ready to work. It would have been disaster to have the people all ready to get started on the work after such a rousing speech and then not have any specific plans laid out as to who should do what and where. Nothing will deflate people quicker than to be all geared up for action and have nothing to do. If Nehemiah would not have had his plan for action in hand, it would have taken him much longer to get the people back to the point of action when he did have a plan.

Three Important Words in Motivation

Three words characterize Nehemiah's plan of action as it

unfolds before us in Nehemiah 3:1–32: (1) coordination, (2) cooperation and (3) commendation.

1. Coordination

First, there was coordination in Nehemiah's plan to rebuild the wall. Each person was assigned a particular area of the wall for which he was responsible. The whole third chapter of Nehemiah is filled with phrases like "next to them," "beyond him," "after him." Everyone was assigned a place to work.

2. Cooperation

Second, there was cooperation in that men and women from different places and from different vocations all worked side by side. There were priests and Levites, rulers and common people, gatekeepers and guards, farmers and city people, all working side by side. There were also craftsmen such as goldsmiths and pharmacists as well as merchants, women and temple servants, all working side by side to do the work of the Lord. The work effort was accomplished through their cooperation with one another.

3. Commendation

Finally, there was commendation given to everyone who worked. The names of the people are forever recorded in the Word of God (Nehemiah 3) as a commendation for a job well done. Further, there were others who were given special commendations because they had gone beyond the call of duty. Some were recorded as having "zealousy repaired" their section (3:20); others did more than one section (3:11, 19–21, 24–27, 30); some repaired an extraordinary length of 1,500 feet on the wall (3:13); some worked alone (3:14). All these people were awarded an extra note of commendation.

One final note is due regarding the listing of the names of the people who received commendations for their work. There were those in the congregation that refused to work and their names are also listed for all to see—the nobles of the Tekoites (3:5). Nothing much is said about these nobles as to their reasons for not wanting to participate. One can only assume that since they were of the upper class of the people they felt they were too good to get their hands dirty working on the wall.

There are always people who feel they are too good to degrade themselves in the lower forms of service to the Lord. Some only want to serve the Lord at the forefront, where people can see their accomplishments. Some only want to serve the Lord when it is convenient. Some do not want to serve in situations that are inconsistent with their luxurious lifestyle—and that is their problem. We who are in leadership must always remember the example of the Lord Jesus Christ, who took the lowest position known to people of His day—He took the position of a servant and washed the dirty feet of the disciples (John 13:1-17).

Though these people were the nobles of the Tekoites, they were useless in the service of the Lord. And just as the Lord knows the workers, He also knows the shirkers.

You Must Be Self-Motivated

Just like Nehemiah, the redevelopment pastor must be self-motivated if he is to succeed. His whole motivation for service in the church must be the joy and satisfaction in knowing he has served the Lord and made an impact upon people's lives for eternity. He is doomed to failure if he looks for the praise of men or other extrinsic rewards as primary responses to his ministry. His eyes must be fixed upon the Lord Jesus Christ as his primary source of motivation. There will not often be someone constantly looking over his shoulder to make sure he gets the job done. He must be a self-motivated servant of the Lord.

You Can't Do It All

The redevelopment pastor must also know how to motivate others and enlist their support in the work to which the Lord has called him. He will not be able to do it all by himself; he needs the help and support of the church people.

When he arrives at his new ministry, he must know how to assess the situation in a tactful manner. He must be able to let the people know that he is one of them and wants to bring hope to the church's life. He must be able to point out problems gradually and in such a way that he does not pin the blame for it all on the people. He must let them know that the Lord has a purpose for their church. Then they will desire to transform their declining church into a growing church for the glory of the Lord.

The redevelopment pastor must make sure the people of the church know the Lord is working in his life. Often they cannot see the Lord's hand in their own lives or in the life of the church and they need to see that a man has come in whose life the hand of God is evident. He also needs to let them know that he is genuinely interested in them and their personal welfare. They need to know that he did not come merely to build up his own reputation as a "miracle worker"; they need to know that he loves the Lord and wants them to know and serve Him as he does; they need to know that he wants to see God glorified in their individual lives and also in the corporate life of the church.

The redevelopment pastor needs to have a prayerfully prepared plan in his hands before he stirs the church to action. And that plan must have a meaningful place for every person to serve in accomplishing the overall plan for the church. He must also remember to commend the people for their service and give them signs of recognition for exceptional work done for the Lord. This will spur them onward in their service for Christ and will be a blessing to the life of the church.

Chapter 11

Handling Obstacles in the Ministry— Part 1

[2:9–10; 4:1–23]

Every redevelopment pastor needs to learn how to handle obstacles in his ministry—especially when the declining ministry is turning around and beginning to grow. As long as the work is declining, the devil does not care about its on-going programs, for they will never make an impact for Christ. But the moment he begins to suspect a change in direction for a declining ministry, the devil will always stir up trouble somewhere, either from within or without.

It's Part of the Job

One of the unwritten points in the job description of every spiritual leader is the requirement that he knows how to handle criticism. Criticism is one of the factors that "comes with the territory" of being a spiritual leader. As Chuck Swindoll says,

> Part of the unwritten job requirements for every leader is the ability to handle criticism. That's part of the leadership package. If you never get criticized, chances are you aren't getting anything done. A wise leader will evaluate the opposition in light of the spirit

115

and attitude in which the criticism is given. He will also consider the voice to which the opposition listens. If your critics listen to God's voice, you had better listen to them. But if they are marching to a different drumbeat, use the Nehemiah technique: "Look, they're not even in the same camp. Let's go right on."[1]

How to Handle It

All who seek to be in positions of spiritual leadership need to learn how to evaluate and handle the criticism that is directed toward them. It is not a matter of *if* it comes, but *when* it comes, for getting criticism is part of being a spiritual leader.

Evaluate the Critic

One of the first things that a spiritual leader must do in the face of criticism directed toward him is to evaluate the critic. Does it come from one who loves him as a brother in Christ? Or, is it from one who has a history of being antagonistic toward him? Is this person a growing Christian, or is he carnal? Is this person going through a personal crisis in his own life and his criticism is merely an emotional vent for him without any meaning for you? Who is this person who is criticizing you and what spiritual and emotional state is he in? Sometimes criticism is a cry from the critic to be ministered to. If the spiritual leader does not recognize this, he will miss an opportunity to minister to the critic's real needs.

Evaluate the Criticism

Second, evaluate the criticism. Is what the critic says an accurate perception of what you said or did? Do you need to explain a misunderstanding? Even if what he says is a gross inaccuracy of the situation, the spiritual leader must listen to him to see if the Spirit of God is speaking through the criticism. It might be that his criticism is 98 percent false and two percent accurate, and the spiritual leader must deal with the two percent truth as much as he can.

In Second Samuel 16:5–14, there is an incident in which a man, Shimei, came out to curse David. David's men wanted to "cut off his head," but David knew that it might be that this man had something from the Lord for him to hear. Once he had heard what Shimei had to say, he would evaluate it and learn what he could from it.

In the next chapter ("Handling Obstacles in the Ministry–Part 2"), we will look in detail at how we should handle criticism, but for now, let me give just four brief statements on how the spiritual leader is to view criticism:

1. Try not to take the criticism personally, unless it is directed to you personally.
2. Remember that it is part of the job of a spiritual leader in a growing ministry.
3. Recognize that discouragement comes from the enemy to get you to quit and let him defeat the ministry.
4. See if there are any positive lessons that can be learned from the criticism or the critic.

Principles of Spiritual Warfare

The one receiving the criticism must learn principles of spiritual warfare:

The Warfare Is Spiritual

Paul taught in Ephesians 6:10–12 that the real struggles that the spiritual leader faces in leading the Lord's people into victory and purpose do not come from people and events—though that is where they are manifested—but from the evil one and his allies. If the spiritual leader becomes embroiled in a conflict with a person or an event, he will lose sight of his real foe and of the resources of God for gaining the victory.

God Allows It

Another principle that the spiritual leader must learn is stated in Genesis 50:20, where Joseph told his brothers, "You intended to harm me, but God intended it for good to accomplish what is now being done, the saving of many lives." Though the stated purpose of the devil toward God's people is "to steal and kill and destroy" (John 10:10), he must first go to the Lord God to ask for His permission (Job 1:9–12; Luke 22:31–32). And when the Lord does grant permission to allow the devil to bring something into the Christian's life, the Lord also imposes limitations upon the type, intensity and duration of the temptation (Job 1:12, 2:6; 1 Corinthians 10:13; see also Revelation 2:10). So if the Lord God does allow the devil to afflict the Christian in some way, the Christian can be sure that even though it was of the devil's design, it has God's stamp of approval upon it and that He will use it for His glory and for our benefit (Romans 8:28–29).

It's Unavoidable

No individual who seeks to live for the Lord God (2 Timothy 3:12), nor any ministry that is growing (Acts 6:1), will escape the attention of the devil. He will not sit idly by while the kingdom of God advances. The devil will stir up those whom he can to carry out his attacks upon God's people and God's work.

Anyone who wants to have an impact upon his world for the Lord Jesus Christ must be prepared to pay his dues. Effective spiritual leadership has a price to be paid and the greater the impact the greater the price. Those in spiritual leadership must have a thick skin but a tender heart. They will be objects of criticism; and they need to know how to handle the hurts that come with the job, if their work for the Lord is to last.

External Obstacles That Nehemiah Faced

Whenever a ministry begins to show signs of spiritual life, we can expect the devil to raise up opposition to that ministry. Sometimes that opposition will come in the form of external pressures or conflicts. Sometimes that opposition will come in the form of internal turmoil or friction between members. And when these forms of opposition do not win out, they increase and return until the enemy knows he cannot bring defeat and kill the now-growing ministry. And even after that he will still seek to bring in forms of opposition for his disruptive purposes.

We have examples of the devil's activity like this from the book of Acts. In chapter four, the church was opposed from the outside. In chapter five, there was internal friction. Both forms only spurred the young church on to an even greater ministry. In chapter six, there was murmuring from within the church and the beginning of opposition from without which ultimately resulted in Stephen's being martyred. When the scattering of the church took place in chapter eight, the devil must have realized he would not kill this new church; yet he still took measures from that point on to be disruptive in it to take away its testimony and effectiveness in the world.

How to Handle Ridicule, Scorn and Doubt

The first recorded act of opposition that Nehemiah faced from outside sources was the ridicule, scorn and doubt about Nehemiah's loyalty to the king, as given in Nehemiah 2:19: "They mocked and ridiculed us. 'What is this you are doing?' they asked. 'Are you rebelling against the king?' " These people knew that a few years before, this same accusation had been sufficient to stop the work (Ezra 4:13). They hoped that threatening to tell the king again what was happening would discourage the people. However, Nehemiah was on the scene now and he was not about to let them stop the work through unfounded accusations. Their insinuation that Nehemiah was leading the Jews into rebellion was totally unfounded and they knew it. They knew why he had come and that he had come with the king's blessing (Nehemiah 2:8).

Sanballat, Tobiah, and Geshem made their accusations based upon the Jews' legal right to rebuild the walls and Nehemiah answered their unfounded remarks according to three legal aspects: "you have no share in Jerusalem or any claim or historic right to it" (2:20). His reply was swift and to the point and they knew exactly what he was saying and that he was right in saying it. He left them with no reply. We can only assume that they recognized that Nehemiah was a leader with backbone; he could not be intimidated with their flimsy accusations.

No Share

The first thing that Nehemiah let them know was that they had no share in Jerusalem. That is, they were not Jews and what the Jews did in Jerusalem was none of their business.

No Claim

Second, Nehemiah told the three that they had no claim in Jerusalem. In this statement Nehemiah reminded them that they never had any previous activities in Jerusalem. A memorial is anything that is erected in a given location to provoke a recollection of a previous event. In essence, Nehemiah was saying that they had not previously had any interest in Jerusalem, and he now questioned their sudden change of interest.

No Right

Finally, he told them they had no right in the matter. Nehemiah was the official governor of the area, appointed by the king himself. Nehemiah was the only one who had a right to say what did or did not happen in Jerusalem, not them.

Nehemiah also gave them the basis on which he had come to Jerusalem. When Nehemiah replied to the trio, he stated that his authority for being in Jerusalem and for doing what he was doing was from the "God of heaven" and that they were His servants. Nehemiah wanted even his enemies to know that his calling to Jerusalem to the work of rebuilding the walls and of bringing revival to the people of God in Jerusalem was from God and not merely from the king.

Something else very significant about this part of Nehemiah's response is that it placed the whole task in a new perspective. And more significantly, he announced it all in front of the Jews as well as those who were their antagonists. By Nehemiah's telling them that the authority for the work came from the Lord God, it took the responsibility for success out of his hands and out of the hands of the Jews and made it something that would come from the hand of God. It was His work and they were His servants. They would complete the work if He wanted it completed and stop the work if He wanted it stopped. Completion and success rested not in their hands, but in the hands of the Lord God.

Nehemiah knew that, if he allowed Sanballat, Tobiah and Geshem to spew out their unfounded accusations without challenging them, it would have a detrimental effect upon the morale of the people. The redevelopment pastor must also deal with accusations that threaten the morale of the people with whom he is working. Nehemiah knew the proverb "Drive out the mocker, and out goes strife; quarrels and insults are ended" (Proverbs 22:10). Those who would offer ridicule and scorn from the outside need to be told swiftly and forcefully, as Nehemiah did, that what the church is doing has nothing to do with them and they have no part in it.

One final note has to do with the timing of the ridicule that the three brought up. It came just as the people were aroused to build. The devil never fails to try to bring defeat at the onset of a revival among God's people.

How to Handle Mockery

A second type of attack that Nehemiah and his people experienced was that of mockery (Nehemiah 4:1–3). Donald Campbell notes that "Sanballat was furious when he observed the progress on the wall, because a secure and independent Jerusalem would undermine his authority and might even mean economic loss for Samaria if trade were attracted to the restored city."[2] Sanballat was also filled with indignation that his personal influence, which had been put forth publicly to halt the work, had failed. He was used to people doing what he wanted, and public knowledge of his failure was a great humiliation to him. With this in mind, Sanballat and his friends began psychological warfare on Nehemiah and the people of Jerusalem. The three of them came to the Jews working on the wall and began making degrading statements about the workmanship.

Nehemiah's response to their mockery was much different than his reply to the scorn which he had previously encountered; the mockery was left answered. Being familiar with the Scriptures, Nehemiah must have known Proverbs 26:4, "Do not answer a fool according to his folly, or you will be like him yourself." Instead of answering the folly of their mockery, Nehemiah took the matter to the Lord in prayer (4:4–5).

Many have a problem with Nehemiah's prayer in that he asked God to "turn their insults back on their own heads. Give them over as plunder in a land of captivity." He further asked the Lord *not* to forgive them for what they had done. This is a startling contrast to the New Testament stance of love and forgiveness for one's enemies.

In viewing Nehemiah's response, there are two things we need to keep in mind. First of all, God had promised that those who blessed His people would be blessed and those who cursed His people would be cursed (Genesis 12:3). Nehemiah was only asking God to do what He had promised to do for His people. A second factor to consider was the dispensation in which the request was made. The request came during the dispensation of the law and that makes it even more difficult for us who live under the dispensation of grace to understand how Nehemiah could make such a request. But in the context of the promises of God and the time of the dispensation, the request was a natural thing to make.

How to Handle Threats

When the three adversaries saw that their scorn and mockery had no effect at all on the progress of the walls, they stepped up their attacks. This time they let it be known that they were thinking about coming to Jerusalem to physically fight against the Jews and to try once again to hinder the rebuilding of the walls. "Intensified opposition against the will of God calls for an intensified response," Chuck Swindoll has said. "Nehemiah not only heard the opposition, but he also analyzed available data, prayed, and took decisive, practical action."[3]

The threat of a physical attack upon the people caused Nehemiah to go to the Lord God in prayer and to set a watch around the clock. Here, once again, Nehemiah demonstrated his ability to live a balanced Christian life of faith and works. He committed the whole situation to the Lord God in prayer and he set a watch on the wall to be on the lookout for the oncoming attackers. Prayer is never a substitute for action. Prayer should precede action, but God will not do for us what he expects us to do for ourselves (see Joshua 5:12). Nehemiah understood this principle very well and therefore he set a watch on the wall after he had prayed.

How to Handle Deceit

A fourth means of opposition that Nehemiah faced was that of deceit (Nehemiah 6:1–2). The wall had been almost finished at this point; only the doors on the gates remained to be completed. Now Sanballat and his friends realized they needed to make a different approach to the situation in Jerusalem. Sanballat and Geshem went to Jerusalem to meet with Nehemiah in what seemed to be a peace effort.

However, Nehemiah rebuked their efforts and refused to go along with their request; he knew they were masters of deceit and they only had evil on their minds. They knew that the key to Jerusalem's rebuilding effort and the renewal that the Jews were experiencing were due to Nehemiah's leadership. They knew also that, if they could eliminate him and his leadership, things would soon degenerate back to where they were before he came. They were saying, "Let's be friends. We have had our differences in the past, but that's all over now. You have done what we thought you could not do; we were wrong and we admit it. But like it or not, we are neighbors and we have to get along. Now let's get together and settle our differences."

Nehemiah saw through their plot. He knew that if he went with them to the plain of Ono, just outside the borders of Judah, that it would be easy for them to assassinate him and thereby halt the rebuilding of Jerusalem. Campbell describes the proposal:

> The invitation was to attend a summit conference of
> sorts, in a neutral location near Joppa, between Ash-
> dod and Samaria and outside the borders of Judah.
> Their plausible purpose seemed to be to plan for a
> peaceful coexistence, to resolve their differences so
> that all parties involved could live togeter in mutual
> understanding. But there was a hidden agenda. The
> real purpose of the proposed conference was to lure
> Nehemiah away from Jerusalem to where his assas-
> sination would be easier. With this dynamic leader off
> the scene, the morale of the Jews would sag, the work
> would stop, and the enemies would gain control.[4]

Although the wall was almost completed, the most important part of Nehemiah's mission had yet to begin—that of
reestablishing God's testimony among the people. But
Nehemiah knew of their evil plan and the consequences it
would bring. Just because an enemy offers a peace plan does
not obligate the man of God to receive it without question or
demonstration of its validity.

There were probably some who thought—like some today—
that Nehemiah was being unreasonable. To what extent do
you trust an enemy when he appears with an "olive branch"
in his hand, especially one who has demonstrated hostility
toward you in the not-too-distant past?

Discernment Is Needed

God gives a "sixth sense" to leaders to keep them from
danger. It is this sense of discernment that is so necessary for
all spiritual leaders to possess in order to protect the people
they are responsible for before the Lord God. Such distractions often seem to tempt the leader just when the work is
beginning to make progress. Others would have gone along
with the request and sought to settle things so they could live
in peace together, but not Nehemiah. It takes courage to
stand up to seemingly commendable intentions, but a leader
knows in his heart that things are not always what they seem
to be. There are times when a leader must say "no," even to

an offer that sounds reasonable and honorable.

The redevelopment pastor must learn to discern the promptings of the Holy Spirit to his own heart. Listening to these promptings and acting accordingly will prevent him from making a grave mistake even in areas where he is unsure why he feels that way. Time is on the spiritual leader's side. If an offer given by a former enemy is valid, it will remain open to future acceptance. If the offer is not valid, it will soon become evident upon its rejection. As the events of the situation moved on, Nehemiah's suspicions were proven to be accurate.

Nehemiah's reply to their overtures was an emphatic NO— in diplomatic language. He did not want to go down to them, because his first priority was to finish the city wall, precisely the work they detested so much. Nehemiah was cordial, yet firm, but they did not take "no" for an answer. Four times they repeated their request, but to no avail. Nehemiah was determined to stay out of trouble. "This repeated message of the enemies was a sign of their desperation," F. Charles Fensham observes. "They were trying anything to stop the work on the wall. Jealousy played a not unimportant role in their reactions."[5]

Nehemiah could not be deceived and he wanted nothing to do with those who were deceptive. He knew his first priority was the completion of the walls around Jerusalem, so he could move on to the second phase of his ministry.

When repeated pressures are placed on a person, his mettle is tested. Weaker men bow to the pressures around them, but Nehemiah would not be distracted, nor would he be swayed by letters from Sanballat. The redevelopment pastor needs to maintain his close walk with the Lord Jesus so that he will be able to sense in his spirit when not to submit to an offer of peace which is meant for his destruction.

How to Handle Rumors

When the four letters sent to Nehemiah failed to bring him to the plain of Ono, Sanballat sent one of his servants to read a letter to Nehemiah openly so all the other Jews working on the wall could hear also. The intended purpose of the letter was to start a damaging rumor among the people and thus put public pressure on Nehemiah. Barber comments:

> The libel may be totally false, yet it is impossible for the victim of such calumny ever to clear his name with everyone who gives ear to the reports. The implication of Nehemiah's supposed treasonous activities is nothing less than attempted blackmail. The strength of their scheme lies in man's innate fear of reprisal. To anyone less heroic, their diabolic threat would have been overwhelmingly powerful. Nehemiah, however, faced their innuendo with commendable courage."[6]

In the letter, Sanballat pretended to be Nehemiah's friend and was telling him of some rumors that he had heard floating around. Sanballat intended the contents of the letter to sound like he was merely reporting to him what he had heard; he wanted to come across as an innocent bystander in it all. But Nehemiah knew him for what he was: the originator of the rumor and the one who wanted to spread it around for the maximum mileage he could get out of it.

Two Characteristics of a Rumor

There are usually two characteristics of a rumor:

1. The source of the rumor is never revealed. This way the one hearing the rumor cannot evaluate the message in terms of the source. Nor can one go to the source to verify the message or to challenge the contents. One good means of discerning between that which is fact and that which is rumor is to identify the source. If the source cannot be identified, it is most likely a mere rumor.
2. The message is usually exaggerated and inaccurate. Anyone who has played the game where people sit in a circle and one whispers a message in one person's ear and then passes it on to his neighbor, and so on, knows how distorted a message can get in a short

period of time. The further a rumor is from the true source, the greater its degree of exaggerations and inaccuracies.

People who live outside the abundant life of the Christian—lost people as well as carnal Christians—are attracted to rumors. They appeal to their fallen, sinful nature; the rumor-monger is secretly built up by hearing of another's downfall. But rumors and false reports will backfire on those who pass them on (Proverbs 26:17–28).

The rumor that Sanballat spread had both of the above characteristics—an unknown source and false information.

Unknown Source

The notable thing about the source of this rumor was that although it was unknown, it seemed to be verified by Geshem, a crony of Sanballat and tribal chief of Kedar in northern Arabia. His name was probably added to give the rumor a sound of credibility or importance. Sanballat probably doubted that Nehemiah would meet with him and Geshem to dispel the rumor. But if he did, they could assassinate him on the way. The rumor was untraceable, though it may have had its source in Geshem's earlier encounter with Nehemiah (2:19).

False Information

The second aspect of a rumor was also seen in Sanballat's letter; it contained gross inaccuracies. Someone had reported to Sanballat that Nehemiah had hired "prophets" to proclaim him king in Jerusalem. What was the source of this rumor? Perhaps it was fueled by a misinterpretation of the book of Zechariah, which predicted the rebuilding of Jerusalem (8:3–5) and also speaks of the Messiah coming to rule and reign as King (9:9). Was Sanballat accusing Nehemiah of claiming to be the Messiah? Whenever one is looking for something to hold against another, he will always be able to find something to satisfy his hatred. Angry, bitter people hear only what they want to hear.

The way in which Nehemiah handled this situation was very simple; he merely denied the accusation and then took the matter to the Lord God in prayer. There is no way to stamp out a rumor once it has been let out. One can only take the matter to the Lord in prayer and trust Him to work things out. He may check out the source to clear up any misunderstanding, but ultimately others will choose to believe that which is false over that which is true. Those who are carnal will receive the rumor and those who are spiritual will reject the rumor.

The spiritual leader in a growing ministry must learn how to handle obstacles or he will be defeated by them and the work of the Lord Jesus Christ will suffer for it. The pastor who sets his heart on fire for Jesus must learn to get used to the heat that comes with it all.

Chapter 12

Handling Obstacles in the Ministry— Part 2

[5:1–6:19]

There are no simple steps to follow in handling all the external obstacles that come before the spiritual leader. There are, however, some factors that affect how the leader handles the criticism and other difficulties.

One of the greatest factors that affects how we handle these outside obstacles is how we view the sovereignty of God. If we feel that God is always in control of all things at all times, then we will be more comfortable with the concept that whatever obstacle we face in our ministry has been allowed by God for a purpose, and that it will ultimately bring Him glory and we also will benefit from it.

Variable Factors Affect How We Handle Criticism

Humanly speaking, there are several other factors that will affect how we handle criticism. In his book *Potshots at the Preacher*, James Allen Sparks lists for us six, which are given here in condensed form:

1. How you feel about yourself at the moment you receive criticism is crucial to how you are likely to accept it.

2. Another factor that influences how we take criticism is how sensitive we are to our own inadequacies. Criticism that strips us naked, revealing our blemishes, becomes crisis-provoking, and our response is more survival-oriented than growth-oriented.

3. How entwined one's self-worth is to the role he or she performs affects how one accepts criticism.

4. Your response to criticism in the past may affect your present attitude toward it and how you receive it.

5. The situational context—physical setting, timing, and support processes—out of which criticism comes is important in whether we perceive it as helpful or diminishing.

6. How we perceive the power of the one who is giving the criticism is a determining factor in how we receive their criticism.[1]

"I Don't Mean to Criticize, But . . ."

When the spiritual leader recognizes that he is about to receive some criticism, he needs to take stock of his concept of the sovereignty of God and his own emotional condition at the time. Additionally, the spiritual leader can take other steps when he knows he is about to receive criticism. He should, if at all possible, make the first move. Contact the individual and let him know that you have heard he is dissatisfied either with you or with something you have done. This takes away the critic's element of surprise and immediately puts you in control of the situation.

Ask for a brief description of the criticism. Once that has been given to you, make an appointment with the critic for a set time, not to exceed 45 minutes (give a beginning time and an ending time—"I could meet with you from 7:00 to 7:30 p.m. on Tuesday"), and no sooner than three days later. This has two advantages:

- it gives you time to do any needed research on the situation;
- it gives the critic time to cool off.

Often, once a critic is forced to reduce the criticism to a brief statement, and is also given time to think it over, the vast majority of steam in the situation is taken away. If not, when the critic comes for the appointment, be sure to let him know of your interest in getting to the bottom of the issue and genuinely resolving it. Listen to what the critic says, take notes on everything, and root out the source of every comment ("Several people think . . ." "Who are they by name?" "I was told . . ." "Who told you?"). If the critic will not identify such sources, then terminate the appointment graciously because he is not genuinely interested in resolving anything. He only wants to lay blame on whoever is the subject of the criticism. If he does identify sources of information, state that you would like to check out what was said from each of them and that you will identify the critic as your source of where you received their name and the information in question. Often critics and criticism have left the realm of logic, so if the matters are pursued logically, the critic will be forced to either resolve the matter or take other steps of evasive action.

How to Handle Obstacles from Within

It is not a matter of whether or not the spiritual leader will face obstacles in his ministry; that is a given assumption. The issue is whether or not he can receive benefit from all that the Lord God has for him in allowing the situation to come about.

While some obstacles come from external sources, other obstacles will come from internal sources, from within the ministry. It is not unusual for those who have been in a declining ministry for a period of time to have several personal problems for which they would like to seek the counsel of the redevelopment pastor once they see that he really is a man of God who can bring them hope and vision for the future. Such was the case with Nehemiah, and such is often the case with the redevelopment pastor after he has been involved in the ministry for some time. After the people have seen him handle some delicate life situations, they will approach him for counsel regarding their own personal problems.

The fifth chapter of Nehemiah records how he handled obstacles to the ministry as they arose from within. Several people in Jerusalem had been feeling a financial crunch in their lives. Some had very large families and did not have enough food to go around for everyone. Others had mortgaged their property in order to endure inflation. Some were heavily in debt and unable to pay any more for anything. The people were in this financial crunch because there was a famine in the land (5:3), there was a heavy tax burden placed upon them by King Artaxerxes (5:4), and the high and inappropriate interest rates were eating away at their resources (5:5, 7). Nehemiah listened to their complaints. The more he listened, the more angry he became at what was taking place. In his plan of correction, he gave us a five-step plan on how to attack anger.

How to be Angry in the Will of God

1. Admit That You Are Angry

The first step in his plan of correction was to admit to himself that he was angry (5:6). Cyril Barber points out that "Even though it was brought about by circumstances over which he had no control, he did not blame others for the way he felt."[2] Many times Christians will not admit they are angry because they feel that such an admission is not consistent with their "Christian testimony." They believe that to be angry is to admit they are not walking in the Spirit. But that is not necessarily so. In Ephesians 4:26, the Bible says, " 'In your anger do not sin': Do not let the sun go down while you are still angry." It is possible to be angry and yet not sin. The Lord Jesus Christ was not happy when He went into the temple to chase out the moneychangers. He was angry at what was taking place (John 2:13–17), and yet we know that He alone was without sin (Hebrews 4:15; 2 Corinthians 5:21). It is possible to be angry in the will of God and Nehemiah tells us how to do it.

Hiding or denying personal anger accomplishes nothing; it does not remedy the situation and it does not help the person feel better. It only allows things to go on as before and make the person go into a "slow boil," which can result in physical problems.

2. Give Yourself Some Space

Once Nehemiah had admitted to himself that he was indeed angry, he was ready to move on to the second stage of the plan: he gave himself space to talk it over with himself and evaluate his anger (Nehemiah 5:7). "The second step is to suppress taking any action until you have thought through the situaton and have control of what you say and do. Suppressing taking action is not the same as repression."[3] Often when we are angry, the natural response is to strike back with an equal or greater intensity than the action that made us angry. But that is the worst thing we can do. We need some time to cool down and think things through. Exercising a measure of self-control will give perspective to the problem that an immediate explosion cannot.

It is interesting to point out that Nehemiah did not talk it over with others; he thought it through himself. He wanted to see if he had a justified reason to be angry. For this he needed time to think things through and to separate his emotional reactions.

Nehemiah was angry because he had come to Jerusalem to rebuild the walls and to restore God's testimony among his people; and yet he knew that if the people did not live in accordance with the teachings of God's Word, they could not enjoy His blessing on their lives, their families or their nation. What he heard from the people revealed that they had broken the law in at least two areas: (1) they could lend other Jews money, but they were not to charge them interest (Exodus 22:25 and Deuteronomy 23:19–20), and (2) they could not permanently enslave another Jewish brother or sister (Leviticus 25:35–40).

3. Confront the Source

The third step in Nehemiah's plan of action was that he confronted those who were the source of his anger (Nehemiah 5:7). Nehemiah knew that sometimes a problem arises between people that is not a substance problem, but a perception problem. That is, a problem that is not truly a problem, but is perceived to be a problem by one or more people. And the only way to see if there really is a problem is to confront the people who are the primary source and talk out what they perceive to be a problem. It might be a simple misunderstanding or a misinterpretation of what was said, or it could be that there are some missing facts that could explain the situation. But we will never know if there really is a problem, or just a perception of a problem, unless we talk to those who ignited our anger.

It is so easy to brood instead of taking steps to correct a problem. Once he thought about it, Nehemiah decided to go to the ones who were getting rich at their brothers' expense.

4. Seek Restoration

The fourth step of restoration is closely related to the third step of confrontation. Not only did Nehemiah approach those who were the source of his anger and bring the charges face to face, but he also brought corrective steps of action for them to implement (5:10–13).

Sometimes those who feel they are more spiritual than they really are think it is their duty to expose sin in the lives of the people around them. But the Scriptures lay a heavier responsibility upon those who are spiritual than the mere exposure of error. Galatians 6:1 tells us, "Brothers, if someone is caught in a sin, you who are spiritual should *restore* him gently. But watch yourself, or you also may be tempted" (italics added). There is no virtue in mere exposure, but the one who is spiritual will seek to restore the individual to rightness. When Nehemiah approached the people involved, he brought biblical solutions to the problems.

Nehemiah told them to stop charging interest to their brothers (Nehemiah 5:10) and to stop enslaving the Jews on a permanent basis (5:11). He also asked them to make a vow before God (5:12) to uphold the scriptural position in the practical, financial matters of their lives and he impressed upon them the serious nature of the vow before the Lord God.

5. Set an Example

Nehemiah concludes chapter five with the best way to handle internal obstacles to the ministry. He demonstrated the life that he expected others to live. This is just as true for the redevelopment pastor or any other spiritual leader.

Nehemiah did this in three ways:

1. He did not demand his rights to the salary that was his (5:14).
2. He did not get distracted from the purpose for which he came to Jerusalem (5:16).
3. He demonstrated a giving lifestyle (5:17).

These are qualities that must be seen in the life of every spiritual leader, especially the redevelopment pastor, if he is to lead his people into a new experience with the Lord Jesus Christ.

One Other Obstacle

There was one other incident at the end of chapter six (6:10–19) that is a common temptation in the ministry for the redevelopment pastor. When the redevelopment pastor faces times of great pressure in his ministry, the enemy tries to make him react under that pressure and violate the principles of Scripture. Nehemiah saw right through that tactic and would not compromise his standards because he knew what the Word of God said.

When his critics saw that they were unable to get Nehemiah outside the city walls to kill him (probably by making it look like an accident), they had to do something inside the city. Nehemiah received a note from a prophet named Shemaiah saying he wanted to meet with Nehemiah right away (Shemaiah proved later to be a false prophet who had been bribed by Sanballat and Tobiah).

When Nehemiah got to Shemaiah's home, Shemaiah told him that he had a message for Nehemiah and that they should meet in the temple to talk about it. The message, briefly, was that Shemaiah had heard of a plot to kill Nehemiah and he wanted Nehemiah to flee to the temple for safety. But Nehemiah was able to see right through this falsehood immediately. "Since it was apparent that the enemy could not lure him outside the wall, they would attack him within the city," comments Richard H. Seume. "In order to expedite their new attack, they bribed Shemaiah, one of Nehemiah's own kinsmen within the city of Jerusalem, to meet with him in the temple under the pretense that his life was in danger."[4]

The real purpose behind this offer was to put Nehemiah in a compromising situation. If he had yielded to this request, his enemies would have exposed him as a man governed by fear and cowardice, thus undermining Nehemiah's influence. They also would have undermined his religious convictions since he was a layman, and as such was not permitted by the law to enter the temple; only priests could do that. Nehemiah knew that violating the restriction would carry the penalty of death (Numbers 18:7).

Nehemiah's knowledge of the Scriptures kept him from falling for the plot and into sin. It was bad enough that Sanballat and Tobiah were trying to assassinate him; he did not need to be disciplined by the Lord for breaking the Word of God. Nehemiah understood that it is never right to do wrong; it is never permissible to break the principles of the Word of God, even when it seems the most logical thing to do.

The encounter left Nehemiah with a heartfelt need to pray that the Lord would not forget those who tried to deceive him.

A Man with a Different Agenda

Nehemiah's enemies misjudged him. They evaluated him by how they themselves would have acted, according to their own standards. They also minimized the importance of Nehemiah's practical, working faith. It was not merely a theoretical theology; it was a living, active faith.

The lesson for the redevelopment pastor here is that he should be most careful in pressure-filled circumstances not to feel forced into a situation that would cause him to compromise his convictions. The redevelopment pastor will soon learn that the Lord will lead him, but the devil will drive him. Learning to distinguish the leading from the driving will save him from being forced into a situation where he would act rashly. The devil will use all sorts of tactics to make the leader compromise in the early stages of the work, but the redevelopment pastor cannot do what he knows to be wrong and expect the Lord God to continue to bless his ministry.

The redevelopment pastor needs to be aware that he is on the front lines in a spiritual war. He must know his enemy and the various tactics he uses. More important, he must know his Lord and walk in His Word.

Chapter 13

Training Faithful Men for Leadership

[7:1–73]

Nehemiah had two goals in mind when he came to Jerusalem (Nehemiah 1:2). His first goal was to rebuild the wall surrounding Jerusalem. The accomplishment of this goal would provide for the protection of the city from marauders and reestablish the testimony of the Lord God among the nations. Jerusalem was known as the city of God and the heathen nations around Jerusalem knew how the Jews viewed their God by the condition of the city. Now that the city walls had been completed (7:1), it was time to move on to the second goal. As Donald K. Campbell observes, "Yet, though the walls had been restored, Nehemiah did not consider his work to be at an end. His deep concern now was for people, for they too needed restoration."[1]

The redevelopment pastor needs to do as Nehemiah did—have a second goal fully developed and ready to be implemented when the first goal is completed. If new goals are not established, the people fall back into chaos. People, especially in a declining ministry, need a common goal to promote growth and a sense of community. Experienced spiritual leaders know the value of keeping realistic goals before their people. This sense of common direction builds unity in and loyalty to the group. Achieving those goals brings a great amount of satisfaction to the people and encourages them to evaluate their progress and move onward in the work of the Lord.

The second goal that Nehemiah had in mind was to rebuild the people. He wanted to establish qualified leadership (chapter 7), bring revival to the people (8, 9, 10), and provide for the ongoing city of God (11, 12). With the first goal—repairing the walls—completed, Nehemiah gave himself wholly to the completion of the second goal—rebuilding the lives of the people.

The Great Need for Faithful Men

The first stage in the pursuit of the second goal was to seek out faithful men to train for the ministry. For 52 days, Nehemiah had the opportunity to observe all the men of Jerusalem as they worked on the wall. This was an important step in the process of building a strong ministry out of a declining ministry. As the men worked on the wall, Nehemiah was able to see who had leadership potential—men who were self-starters, men who paid attention to the details of their work, men who went beyond what was expected, men who had a teachable spirit, men who joined Nehemiah in prayer when opposition came. These men were to become the leaders in whom Nehemiah would invest his life to strengthen the ministry.

This is also the pattern that the redevelopment pastor needs to follow when he first comes to the declining ministry to begin his work. He needs to map out a plan to work on the physical facilities on which the whole church can work together. This will give him the opportunity to see who are the true workers in the church, both of the men and of the women. Once he knows who has leadership potential, he can direct his efforts toward building them up in the faith and equipping them for ministries. It is not at all unusual that the real leaders in the church are not those who hold the official positions; this is one probable reason why the church became a declining ministry in the first place.

Some would take exception to the redevelopment pastor giving himself primarily to the ones who have demonstrated their faithfulness to the work of the ministry and have leadership potential. Some would say that the pastor should work with all people equally and not give such concentrated attention to certain ones in the church. They would say that we need to encourage those who are on the fringe of the church and try to get them to become more faithful to the work. Though these statements sound good, and even have a spiritual tone to them, they are biblically unsound and highly impractical if the redevelopment pastor is going to turn the declining ministry into a growing ministry.

Why Train Only the Faithful?

Why should the redevelopment pastor train only the faithful men for ministry and not everyone equally? There are several reasons:

Relationship Between Leadership and Growth

The reason most ministries decline in the first place is because the men are not committed to the Lord and to the work. In *Dynamics of Church Growth*, Ron Jenson and Jim Stevens describe this relationship between leadership and growth:

> A ministry will rise or fall on its leadership. To the extent that a church can reproduce spiritual, effective leadership, it can enjoy Biblical growth. The inability to develop such leadership is a major source of stagnation. Without this leadership there is no one to equip the rest of the laity to be involved in the ministry, and there is no corporate small group which models a lifestyle that creates a thirst within the church people—a desire to become bright lights and salt.[2]

No ministry will grow if it does not have committed leadership or the ability to reproduce leaders. Seeking to train those who are not committed to the Lord and to the ministry in question will only lead to decline once again in the very near future.

There are two biblical models in the training of leaders:

1. In Exodus 18:13–27, Jethro counseled his son-in-law, Moses, to select "capable men" (18:21) and place them in positions of ministry. The Hebrew word *chayil*, translated here as "capable," is used to note one who has personal strength or might or power. It is a word that can be used in the physical sense or in the moral sense and the precise meaning is determined by the context. In this case, Jethro was counseling Moses to choose men who had proven moral strength and place them into the positions of leadership. Further, Moses was to give instruction to these men as to what their exact responsibilities were to be. Moses was not to give his time and efforts to just any man, but only to the man of proven moral character.

2. Again, in Ephesians 4:11–12, the Scriptures say that one of the reasons that God has given some to be pastor-teachers in the church is to "prepare God's people" so that they can do the work of the ministry and build up the body of Christ. This Greek word for "people" (*hagios*) has a twofold moral and spiritual sense to it. It means one who is separated from sin and therefore consecrated unto the Lord God. In his pulpit and counseling ministries, the pastor seeks to lead his people to live their lives consecrated unto the Lord God. And when they do, then he is to give them more specific, intense training to be ministry leaders in the body of Christ. But not until they have demonstrated that they are serious about the things of God for their lives can this happen.

In each of these biblical cases, spiritual leaders are exhorted to concentrate their efforts on the true workers in the ministry—those who have demonstrated teachability and leadership potential—and not just anyone. It is the responsibility of every

Christian to become involved in a ministry that utilizes his spiritual gifts, abilities and talents. And it is the responsibility of the church leadership to equip the faithful ones to do the work of the ministry that the Lord has given each to do.

The Danger of Lowered Standards

There is another reason training faithful men is important: when those on the fringe of spiritual living are sought to be trained for ministry, those who are already committed to the Lord and His work are tempted to become lax in their own commitment and the whole ministry suffers in the long run.

Further, when a person who is content to live on the fringe is given a responsibility in the ministry, it will not change his commitment level; someone who is not committed on the fringe will not be committed in a place of ministry.

This also has another detrimental effect. It tells everyone the standard by which we are governed. Kenneth Gangel warns that "A minimizing of the standards of excellence in local church leadership contributes to the problem of worker recruitment. Not many people want to work for a shoddy organization."[3] When the standards for leadership are lowered to include those who have not demonstrated themselves to be the faithful in the church, it not only produces a shoddy ministry, but it lowers the morale of those who are faithful. Besides, who wants to be part of a church where mediocrity is the standard for leadership? High standards not only give the best ministry results, but they attract other Christians who also hold high standards for their own lives.

We cannot sing, "Give of your best to the Master," and then let one who has little or no spiritual qualifications be in a position of leadership. To turn a declining ministry into a growing one, the redevelopment pastor must establish at the very onset a high standard of expectations for those who serve in positions of leadership. And he should expect that some in the church will not be pleased with this. After all, a declining ministry is not known for its high standards, especially in its leadership. But if the pastor stands firm in his convictions, leaders with those high standards will gradually emerge and the church will profit greatly from their impact.

Faithful Men Are Motivated Men

As mentioned in chapter 10, there are two types of motivation for doing the things we do: extrinsic and intrinsic. Extrinsic motivation means that one must be constantly prodded on by external rewards in order to keep going; he must be motivated by rewards to start and finish a task. Intrinsic motivation means that one finds joy and reward within the accomplishment of the task involved. People who are intrinsically motivated will be able to give themselves wholeheartedly to a task and enjoy doing their best in whatever they do. They do not need to be prodded on by others or by rewards. Only those who are intrinsically motivated (i.e., faithful men) will ever be able to give their all for the Lord's work.

A Biblical Guideline

Another reason to concentrate on the faithful has to do with the biblical guidelines for those who are to be spiritual leaders, primarily in a declining church ministry. It is my firm conviction that no declining church ministry will ever become a growing ministry until the *men* of the church begin to get serious about the things of God and become committed to Him and His work in this lost world. It is also the emphasis of the Scriptures that men take up positions of leadership in the work of the Lord's church (1 Timothy 3:1; Titus 1:6; Acts 6:3). This is not to say that women do not have a vital ministry within the church; this is not the issue in this discussion. The point is that only faithful men will make a declining ministry a growing ministry.

Training faithful men is the method Jesus Christ Himself used (Mark 3:14; John 2:23–25). There were the multitudes that Jesus preached to and taught, but out of the multitudes He chose 12 men to be with Him and to train for ministry. He chose the men not for their spiritual maturity, but for their leadership potential because they were self-starters. William Barkley put it this way:

Judging them by worldly standards the men Jesus chose had no special qualifications at all. They were not wealthy; they had no special social position; they had no special education; they were not trained theologians; they were not high-ranking churchmen and ecclesiastics; they were twelve ordinary men. But they had two special qualifications. First, they had felt the magnetic attraction of Jesus. There was something about him that made them wish to take him as their Master. And second, they had the courage to show that they were on his side.[4]

Jesus chose 12 men and poured Himself into their lives for three and a half years. Those men in turn went out and turned the world upside down for Jesus Christ (see Acts 17:6). It was Jesus' intensive training of His men that made the difference. It was not merely academic, but the communication of one life to another. J. Oswald Sanders describes it:

> It remains to be said that the training of leaders cannot be done by employing the techniques of mass production. It will require patient and careful instruction and prayerful and personal guidance of the individual over a considerable period. Disciples are not manufactured wholesale. They are produced one by one, because someone has taken the pains to discipline, to instruct and enlighten, to nurture and train one that is younger.[5]

If we are to have a world-shaking impact upon our area just as the disciples did, we must give ourselves to seeking out faithful men and training them for ministry.

This training of faithful men was also the method that the Apostle Paul used and exhorted others in leadership to use. "And the things you have heard me say in the presence of many witnesses entrust to reliable (faithful, KJV) men who will also be qualified to teach others" (2 Timothy 2:2). Wherever Paul went he was training faithful men for service, and when they were ready, he gave them opportunity for service.

The redevelopment pastor must also give himself to the training of faithful men in order to build the declining ministry into a growing one. Even if he has only one faithful man to work with, he must train that man before the Lord will give him others to work with.

The Call to "Make Disciples"

Finally, there is what we call the Great Commission in Matthew 28:19–20: "Go . . . , make disciples . . . , baptizing them . . . , and teaching them to obey everything I have commanded you." The Lord Jesus Christ taught His disciples *content* by the things He spoke to them. He also taught them *methods* by the way He taught and how He taught. He taught by investing Himself in the lives of 12 men, not by trying to reach the masses. He knew that the way to reach the masses was by multiplying His life in the lives of faithful men who could also reach others.

The leader who is only interested in turning in a numerically inspiring annual report will not choose Jesus' method. But the leader who wants to change the world and make an eternal impact upon it for Jesus Christ will give himself to the making of disciples, the training of "reliable men who will also be qualified to teach others" (2 Timothy 2:2).

How to Select Faithful Men

In identifying potential leaders, Ted Engstrom has some wise counsel:

> It is well said that leaders learn to be leaders. This means that time must be allowed for learners to develop. Before this can happen a group must have some kind of plan to find the best prospects. Random selection seldom brings good results, for if a person really has no potential ability, he should not be considered. Prospects should display some positive attitudes toward the group and give some strong

evidence that he will be able to learn a new task that requires greater skill. Recognition of leadership ability is vital.[6]

Previously we considered some ways in which the redevelopment pastor can do as Nehemiah did and see the faithful men of his congregation emerge as they work on a physical project. But there are also biblical principles, some of which were not available to Nehemiah, that are helpful in selecting faithful men in whom the redevelopment pastor can begin to invest and multiply his life.

Is He Bearing Fruit?

One of the first biblical principles to spot a faithful man is to look at those whose lives are already bearing fruit for the Lord Jesus Christ. In Numbers 17, there was a question about who was really God's choice in the area of leadership for His people. The way He chose to reveal His choice of leadership in this instance was to have each man write his name on a rod and place it in the tabernacle. The next morning God would reveal His choice for leadership; the one whose rod had budded was God's choice. The next morning, Aaron's rod bore fruit and so he was God's choice for leadership.

A New Testament principle that corresponds with this testimony in Aaron's case is found in John 15:8, where Jesus said that the way one proves that he is a disciple, or a learner, is that his life bears fruit already. (By "fruit" I mean one who is bearing the fruit of the Spirit [Galatians 5:22–23], the fruit in the lives of others, by salvation or by spiritual growth [Romans 1:13], or the fruit of righteousness, godly character [Hebrews 12:11].)

The redevelopment pastor should first look for those already involved in a particular ministry that have spiritual results—a Sunday School teacher, a person to whom people look for spiritual counsel, etc.

Does He Want to Be Involved?

A second means of spotting a man with leadership potential, or a faithful man, is to observe one who may not have a present ministry, but desires to be involved in some sort of ministry. Scriptures tell us that it is a good thing for a man to desire a place of spiritual leadership (1 Timothy 3:1). When the redevelopment pastor hears a young Christian voice a desire to be involved in spiritual ministries and/or leadership, he should consider giving this one some spiritual guidance and assistance.

The redevelopment pastor can begin with this person by giving him a small task to do with close supervision. After the task is completed successfully, other tasks can be given with greater and greater importance and with less and less supervision. This way the pastor can develop the person's leadership potential without overburdening him at the beginning. As Jenson and Stevens advise, "The best way to determine faithfulness is to gradually move people from minimal responsibility to more significant responsibility. If a person is not dependable and faithful in the small jobs, it is doubtful that he will be in the larger responsibilities."[7]

Does He Identify with Christ?

Third, when the redevelopment pastor spots a man who identifies his life openly with the Lord Jesus Christ (Luke 14:27), this indicates that he is a candidate in whom the pastor can invest part of his life. Perhaps the candidate wants to have a testimony at his place of employment; the people he works with know he is a Christian, but the man does not know how to explain the way of salvation to them or how to answer their questions regarding Christianity. Often the man will come to his pastor and ask him to go speak to the men at work (or to his neighbor or whomever), but it is better for the pastor not to go. Instead, he should train the man himself so that he can work with them.

Not only can the pastor fulfill his job description by training the man (Ephesians 4:11–12), but the man can have a much more effective ministry with those people at work, or that neighbor next door, because he already has a rapport with them and they have a measure of trust in him. Both these things are lacking if the pastor steps into the picture.

Does He Want to Know the Bible?

A fourth candidate for the redevelopment pastor to consider is the man who wants to know the Scriptures and live his life based on biblical principles (John 8:31–32). He may want to know what the Bible has to say about the way he is to lead his family, or what the Bible has to say about finances or some other topic. This is the man whom the pastor should seek out further as one who has leadership potential.

Does He Admire Committed Christians?

Last, the man who has a love for other committed Christians should be challenged that he could have the same Christian life that he admires in another (13:34–35). It is a known principle of life that those whom we admire are the ones we inwardly want to be like. This may be the first step in a desire to make a spiritual impact on the lives of others for Jesus' sake.

Gaines S. Dobbins defines leadership this way:

> Leadership is not a special gift with which a few exceptional persons are endowed. It is a right to be earned, an ability to be learned, a privilege to be won. Requirements must be met; disciplines undergone; hours of study spent; sacrifices made; earnest prayer engaged in; self-will surrendered to God's will; and love and service of self replaced by love and service of others for Christ's sake—guidance from self-interest replaced by guidance of the Holy Spirit.[8]

Four Needs in Leadership

Nehemiah recognized not only the need *for* spiritual leadership, but the needs *of* spiritual leadership. In Nehemiah 7, he demonstrated four needs of spiritual leadership:

The Need for Training

First, there is a need to engage and train other key men to

assume positions of responsibility and leadership (7:1–4). In choosing these leaders, Nehemiah required that they feared God more than they feared man and that they were faithful men (7:2). Fearing God in this context means that they adhered to the Word of God and were quick to obey His leading and His leaders. Also they had an eternal perspective; they wanted to know the Lord in an intimate way. Further, they were faithful men—faithful to the Lord God and faithful to the work of the Lord as Nehemiah had been called to do. They were pliable, available, teachable and dependable men; men God could use. Their character had already been demonstrated. They were not completely mature in their spiritual life, but they were growing; and that was what Nehemiah was looking for in men with potential for leadership. He knew that positions of leadership are not places for the novice, but places to demonstrate a growing, godly character.

In addition, Nehemiah gave them some specific guidelines for their responsibilities (7:3). Leaders in all areas of responsibility need to know exactly what is required of them. Nehemiah knew that the responsibility of those in the upper levels of leadership was to put forth policies, job descriptions and adequate training in order for others to know exactly what they were expected to do. Otherwise, there would be no means of evaluating their performance.

The Need for Openness

The second need that Nehemiah saw and addressed was for openness in the leadership to receive direction from the Lord (7:5–60). In verse five, Nehemiah says that "God put it into my heart" to take a census. When men commune with the Lord, it is not only a qualification for leadership, it is a quality of ministry. We have previously examined Nehemiah's spiritual life and found it to be exemplary, but here we see a new dimension of his walk with the Lord. He was a man who responded positively and immediately to the promptings of the Lord to his heart. A man's spiritual maturity is directly related to the quickness with which he responds to the promptings of the Holy Spirit to his life. Had Nehemiah not responded to the project that God had put upon his heart, that of taking the census, he would not have known the findings it unveiled. If those in positions of spiritual leadership do not listen to and obey the promptings of God to their hearts, there will be important findings they will miss completely.

The Need for Spiritual Qualifications

Third, Nehemiah knew that there is a need to have adequate spiritual leadership qualified for the ministry (7:61–65). In Nehemiah's course of taking the census, some were found in the priesthood who could not validate their ancestry; this was necessary to prove that they were qualified to be in the priesthood.

Since they could not trace their ancestry and thus prove their heritage for the priesthood, Nehemiah had to remove them from office. Nehemiah knew that in order to have spiritual leadership, the men of the priesthood must be qualified by being men of the tribe of Levi. The Lord God could not honor his leadership any further if the qualifications of those men were based upon human sentiment rather than the Word of God. If the people were to achieve and maintain a close, personal walk with the Lord God, they needed qualified leadership in the priesthood. His decision had nothing to do with job performance or ability. It was not a personal issue with Nehemiah; there were no personality conflicts between him and the others. It was purely a matter of qualifications for various roles. This is a powerful lesson (and sometimes painful, too) for those who work with declining ministries; the redevelopment pastor must be extremely careful to make sure no one is placed in a position of spiritual ministry if he or she does not meet the spiritual qualifications which the Word of God lays out. Men who are in positions of leadership, but do not meet the spiritual qualifications will be a source of contention because they will want the church to operate as they do—carnally, apart from the guidance and authority of the Word of God. And men who are in positions of spiritual leadership, but who have openly violated scriptural principles, will never be able to wholeheartedly lead the church into obedience to the same Scriptures they openly violate.

The Need for Support

Finally, Nehemiah saw the need to have adequate support to do the work of the Lord (7:66–73). When all of Israel saw that Nehemiah was serious in this matter of leadership, it placed a new perspective on the whole issue. When they saw that he meant business, they gave to the work. People give to what they see; a shaky, unfounded operation will have financial difficulties. And the opposite is also true. The Scriptures relate how the people gave to the work of the *Lord*. They didn't give to the work of Nehemiah or to the work of Jerusalem; they gave to the work of the Lord. And when God's people support His work with their tithes and offerings, several things begin to happen. The ministry needs are met, the financial needs of the leaders are met, and the people themselves enjoy God's blessings on their lives.

It is no insignificant matter that as soon as the wall was rebuilt, Nehemiah began working on his second goal of building up the people and reestablishing the testimony of God among them. And even more impressive is the fact that when he began building up the people and God's testimony, he began by establishing faithful men in places of leadership—men who had written job descriptions; men who communed with the Lord and were obedient to His promptings; men who were spiritually qualified for the position they held; men who had adequate financial support for themselves and their ministry.

Faithful men in places of leadership is the place to begin in turning a declining ministry into a growing ministry.

Chapter 14

Setting the Stage for Revival

[8:1–10:39]

With the rebuilding of the walls completed and the new leadership appointed within Jerusalem, the timing was right for the second phase of Nehemiah's second goal to begin. The eighth chapter of Nehemiah begins by telling us that the people gathered themselves together "as one man" and desired to hear Ezra read to them the Word of God. It was a voluntary gathering and there was spontaneity about it all. And yet, the recent series of traumatic events had led to their new desire to hear the Word of God.

First, Nehemiah removed from office those who were not qualified to carry out the role of the priesthood. This brought a grave sense of seriousness to the people's thinking.

Second, the people began to give adequate support for the work of the Lord and for His servants. When people give of their finances to the work of the Lord, there has been a change of their heart as well.

Also, Nehemiah mentions that it was the seventh month, Tishri (September to October), and it could be that the people were reminded of other significant events that had taken place during the month of Tishri. Leviticus 23 tells us that the seventh month was the time for three of Israel's holy days: the Feast of Trumpets, the Day of Atonement and the

Feast of Tabernacles. It was also the month in which the ark of the covenant was moved into the temple (2 Chronicles 5:3-5). During Tishri the Jews had fasted and prayed during their period of captivity (Zechariah 7:5). It was also during that month that the first returnees under Zerubbabel had come back to Jerusalem after the captivity (Ezra 3:1ff).

Even today, there are certain times of the year when people seem more open to the things of the Lord, and for the Jews, the seventh month seemed to be one of those times. The stage was then set for revival to come to God's people.

The Goal: Revival!

Revival was what Nehemiah had hoped and prayed would happen to God's people, but bringing revival was a different type of goal than the goal of rebuilding the walls of Jerusalem. Nehemiah could plan and carry out the rebuilding project, but he could not bring revival in the hearts of God's people. Nehemiah could set the stage and prepare the setting, but only God Himself could bring revival as He initiated it and the people allowed it to continue to affect their own personal lives. The change of heart and the ensuing revival that took place, as recorded in Nehemiah 8-10, was the work of God for which Nehemiah and other godly people in Jerusalem had been praying.

In chapter eight, Nehemiah stepped into the background as the people asked Ezra the scribe to read the Word of God to them. In Ezra 7:10, the Scriptures record that Ezra was a man who was committed to teaching Israel the practicalities of the Word of God: "For Ezra had devoted himself to the study and observance of the Law of the LORD, and to teaching its decrees and laws in Israel." One of Ezra's responsibilities as a scribe was to teach the Word of God to the people, and he did not take that responsibility lightly. Nor did he want his teaching to be mere academics. He wanted first of all to make sure that he knew the Word and had personally applied it to his own heart before he would teach it to others. He wanted his teaching to be effective and life-changing. And life-changing teaching of the Word of God is possible because it has first of all changed the life of the one teaching it.

It must be noted here that Nehemiah's leadership was not threatened by bringing in other men to fill leadership roles that he was not able to perform. Nehemiah was not a priest or a Levite or a scribe. Ezra was, and it was Ezra's role to lead the people in the reading of the Word of God. Nehemiah was not one to seek the position of preeminence because he was the leader of the people, nor did he seek the praise of men because he had done what others had failed in doing—finishing the rebuilding of the wall. His successes did not make him proud; he remained the same as he had been all along. Nehemiah was secure in the role that the Lord had given him, and W. Robertson Nicoll commends him for that:

> A finer proof of the unselfish humility of the young statesman cannot be imagined. Though at the height of his power, having frustrated the many evil designs of his enemies and completed his stupendous task of fortifying the city of his fathers in spite of the most vexatious difficulties, the successful patriot is not in the least degree flushed with victory. In the quietest manner possible he steps aside and yields the place to the recluse, the student, the writer, the teacher.[1]

Like Nehemiah, the redevelopment pastor must feel the freedom to bring in others, perhaps with gifts different than his own, to add new dimensions to the ministry. It is good to bring in missionaries for a special missions emphasis. At other times he may want to invite a fellow pastor or Christian worker to hold special meetings. Or, he may want to bring in people skilled in Christian education to help in the training of his Sunday school teachers, club leaders, etc. It is a wise pastor who recognizes that he does not have all the gifts of the Spirit and that he can bring in others to complement his work. One other thing: even if the pastor feels he could do just as well as the speaker being brought in, he needs to do it periodically. A special speaker can say the same things that

the pastor has been saying all along and suddenly it sparks
the mind of the hearer as if it were a new thought. And, there
are some challenges which a special speaker can give to the
people that the pastor cannot.

Three Ingredients to Revival

Revival is *not* like making a cake—you add the ingredients
in correct proportions and follow the baking directions and
presto, you have a cake. There are certain ingredients that
are most generally found in genuine revivals, but it must be
remembered that revival is a work of God and He will bring
it about in His time and when the conditions are right.

1. It must begin with exposure to the Word of God
   which challenges the mind, stirs the heart and affects
   the will.
2. There must be an effective prayer life generated by a
   desire to communicate with the God of the Bible who
   has spoken to you. That prayer life must be one
   focused upon the Lord God Himself, rather than
   upon self or personal needs.
3. There must be new convictions formed as a result of
   the revival that took place in the believer's heart.

Revival Comes through the Ministry of the Word of God

Revival begins when God's people allow the Word of God
to affect their minds with a challenge. This is the course of
events as they begin to unfold in Nehemiah 8:1–8. "The first
major thrust in a genuine revival is the proclamation of
Scripture," Chuck Swindoll says. "The apostles, who set the
pace for the early church, stayed wih God's Word. Even when
growth occurred and vast numbers of people became followers of Christ, those who led this first-century revival never
ventured from the written Word of God."[2]

The people, both men and women, gathered themselves
together at the wall by the Water Gate while Ezra read the

Word of God to them. While Ezra did that, 13 Levites stationed themselves among the people and enabled them to understand the Word that Ezra was reading to them.

Around 6:00 a.m. the people lifted their hands in prayer and they all responded with a corporate "Amen!" and the reading began. These four things indicated that they meant business with the Lord God:

1. The fact that they got up early enough to be assembled by 6:00 a.m. was an indication of their seriousness.
2. They indicated the seriousness of the day by acknowledging their dependence upon the Lord God in prayer.
3. They lifted up their hands. This was a visual way of telling the Lord one of two things. It either expressed their desire for a closer life with the Lord, as a little child raises his arms to indicate to his father that he wants to be picked up and held close. Or, it could have meant that they were lifting up empty hands acknowledging that they were ready to receive from the Lord all that He had for them and that they had nothing but themselves to offer Him.
4. They said "Amen!" This expression merely says "let it be," or "I agree." They were agreeing with the Lord even before He had told them anything. They did not want to argue nor reject anything which He had for them at this point.

A special wooden pulpit had been built for the reading of the Scriptures where Ezra and those who read the Word stood. As the Scriptures were read, the people bowed before the Lord and worshiped Him with their faces to the ground. Whenever God's people gather together to hear the Word of God read or preached, they will worship. Worship is the natural outcome of coming face to face with the Lord God through the ministry of His Word.

As the Scriptures were read, there were 13 other Levites

who mingled among the people and caused them to understand and apply the Word of God which they were hearing
read to them. This was necessary for two reasons:

1. There was a language barrier. H.A. Ironside said, "it
    needs to be borne in mind that, after the captivity,
    Hebrew, as a spoken language, had largely been
    displaced by Aramaic, hence the need of carefully
    explaining the Hebrew words to the waiting people."[3]
2. As the 13 Levites mingled, they helped the people not
    only understand the language, but also to make per-
    sonal applications of the Word of God that was being
    given. The end result was that, as the Scriptures were
    read, the people were taught the application of the
    Word to their own lives.

The redevelopment pastor must take note of this phase of
Nehemiah's plan. As he assumes his duties in a declining
ministry, he must give attention to the physical facilities to
see who the workers and the leaders really are; and he must
see that spiritually qualified people are in positions of leadership in the ministry. He must also give himself to exposing
the people to the Word of God. In a church setting, this would
mean expository preaching from the pulpit, the centrality of
the Bible in the Sunday school classes, and other means of
exposing people to the Word of God, such as home Bible
studies, individual discipleship programs, etc.

Scripture as a Change Agent

People's lives change and a church's ministries change as
they are exposed to the power of the Word of God personally
applied in their lives. If genuine revival is to come, the Word
must be allowed to affect the emotions as people are under
their own conviction of sin from their exposure to the Word
of God (Nehemiah 8:9–12).

As the people listened to the Word of God and understood
its implications for their lives, they became troubled in their
souls. This is the effect that understanding Scripture has upon

our lives. James (1:23–25) tells us that the Scriptures are the mirror of the soul, and that as we look into the mirror of the Word we see our own sinfulness reflected in the holiness of God.

This is what happened to the people of Jerusalem as they heard the claims of God upon their lives, for they wept when they heard the words of the law. They saw themselves as they had never seen themselves before—from the perspective of God's holiness, which reminded them of their own sinfulness and caused them to weep over their own unrighteousness. They were reminded of all the sins they had committed—both their sins of omission (things they should have done, but did not) and their sins of commission (things they should not have done, but did do).

When the Lord God brings sin to our attention, He does not want us to wallow in the pit of conviction forever. The only reason why He brings the conviction of sins to our attention is so that we will be led to repentance. And the only reason why He wants us to repent of our sins is so that we can receive forgiveness of our sins. And in forgiveness comes the grace of God to live for Him in victory and in the strength of the Lord. In the grace of God comes joy in living and spiritual strength.

As First Chronicles 16:27 tells us, "Splendor and majesty are before him; strength and joy in his dwelling place." The world says that confession and repentance of sin reveals weakness; yet the very opposite is true.

Repentance Brings Joy

Joy and strength come from our new standing before God when we experience His forgiveness and get a new measure of grace by which to live. The joy of the Lord is our strength because, when a Christian is forgiven, it makes available to him all the resources of God for his life which were once blocked by sin. Barber defines it this way:

> Joy is not an ethereal "something" that is divorced from reality. Joy becomes a vital part of our ex-

perience when we rejoice in our standing before God.
This takes place as we learn more of what he has done
for us and enter into the reality of what it means to
belong to him and be accepted by him. When this
happens, we experience joy.[4]

The leaders of the people encouraged them to ask for
forgiveness of their sins, as they became aware of them, and
experience the joy of the Lord and the strength that only He
gives. When they did repent and ask for forgiveness, there
was a joyous time of great celebration and feasting in the city.

This is a good reminder not only to the redevelopment
pastor, but also to all of us who proclaim the Scriptures. As
we give out the Word of God, people are often confronted
by the Spirit of God about an area of their life that needs to
be confessed, repented of and forgiven. We must remember
to lead them beyond mere conviction of sin to experience the
joy of forgiveness and a new measure of strength for their
life; to stop short is to proclaim an incomplete message.

The Word Must Reach the Will

The only way lasting effects of revival will be seen is if the
Word of God is allowed to affect the will, causing life principles to be formed and obeyed (Nehemiah 8:13–18). It is all
too common that believers, faced with the claims of Christ
on their lives, will weep over their sinful conditions but make
no lasting changes in their lives. This is an example of revival
striking the emotions, but not being allowed to go onward to
affect the will.

On the second day, the leaders of all the fathers of the
people assembled to study the Scriptures once again. Donald
K. Campbell describes the scene this way:

Though the mass of people returned to their homes
and towns, the heads of families, the priests and
Levites came back to Ezra on the second day to hear
more. By this time, the reading had progressed to
Leviticus 23 and the people were reminded that on

the 15th through the 22nd days of the seventh month
they were to observe the feast of Tabernacles by
dwelling in booths.[5]

When they found out about this truth, they immediately
began making plans to obey the Scriptures on this point. This
act of immediate obedience to the Word of God was very
admirable. They could have had "reason" for not doing it right
away. (There is never a valid reason for not obeying the
principles of the Word of God; man only thinks there is.) After
all, it was the seventh month then, and the time of the Feast
was immediately at hand. They could have reasoned in their
hearts that they did not have enough time to adequately
prepare for such an occasion. They could have further
reasoned that since it had been overlooked for so long that one
more year would not make that much difference. It was to their
great credit that they did not try to reason themselves out of
obeying; they just began to make plans and obeyed what the
Lord God had showed them in His Word. "To obey it required
considerable inconvenience," Ironside comments. "They
might have argued that what Samuel, David, Solomon and
others had overlooked was surely non-essential; but 'they
found it written,' and that settled it for an obedient people."[6]

For seven days the people held the Feast of Booths and they
also read the Word of God. As a result, "their joy was very
great" (8:17).

The redevelopment pastor must demonstrate in his life and
teach in his ministry the need for instant obedience to new
truths found in the Scriptures. Often in declining ministries
biblical principles have either been ignored or unknown and
need to be known and employed. The redevelopment pastor
should also be aware that change is sometimes difficult, even
in a declining ministry, and he should slowly proceed with
caution in the introduction of drastic changes based upon the
implementation of scriptural principles.

Revival Comes from an Effective Prayer Life

The second ingredient in revival is that of an effective

prayer life that has been nurtured by, and grown out of, one's time in the Word of God (9:1–38). For 24 days, the people had been under the ministry of the reading of the Word of God. For those who had been born during the captivity, that was the first time they had been exposed to the Word. Through the living and active Word of God, the Holy Spirit searched their hearts and drew them into prayer. Their prayer involved seven aspects:

1. Confession of Sin

Their prayer began with confession of their sin (9:2–3). Richard H. Seume describes the people's attitude:

> To confess sin while cleaving to it is mockery. None of that was here. So determined were they to lay the axe to the root of the tree, that they rehearsed before God not only their own sins, but those of their fathers as well. This was no superficial work of the flesh; it was a deep exposure of their sin for which they had suffered chastisement.[7]

First they confessed their own sins. As they listened to the Word of God, the Spirit of God brought great conviction to their hearts. One of the ways we know we have met the Lord and have been in His presence is that we become aware of our own personal sin (Isaiah 6:5; Luke 5:8).

Part of the concept of confession of sin is forsaking the sin once it is known. Proverbs 28:13 tells us, "He who conceals his sins does not prosper, but whoever confesses and renounces them finds mercy." Again, in First John 1:9 the Bible tells us, "If we confess our sins, he is faithful and just and will forgive us our sins and purify us from all unrighteousness." The very word translated "confess" means to view sin in the same manner as God views it. If God considers it to be sin, we must consider it to be sin. And what God considers to be sin, He does not embrace. Confession is not the mere voicing of a statement void of personal impact. Inherent in confession of sin is the desire to turn from it and forsake it.

2. God's Majesty

From confession, the people of Jerusalem turned their attention toward the second step of their prayer, centering upon the majesty of God (Nehemiah 9:4-6). They stood to worship the Lord God and praise Him because of His majesty in Creation. They spoke of His power, His dignity and His authority. This is where prayer ought to always begin, with a proper concept of the majesty of God and not any humanistic conception.

3. God's Righteousness

They moved on to the righteousness of God (9:7-8). They spoke of how God had dealt righteously with Abraham in that He had chosen Abraham, moved him out of the land of Ur, given him a new name and a new purpose, blessed him both spiritually and physically and made a covenant with him. The covenant that the Lord God made with Abraham became fundamental to all of God's dealings with Israel. In all His dealings with Abraham, God kept His promises and proved His righteousness to man. "Abraham served as a challenging example for Nehemiah's generation because the patriarch was obedient when God revealed his will," Campbell says. "If the remnant did the same, they too would experience God's blessing. Obedience is always the passport to blessing."[8]

4. God's Greatness

Their prayer described God's greatness (9:9-15). They recounted the greatness of God in the way that He had demonstrated Himself strong from the time they left Egypt to the time they arrived in the Promised Land. They spoke of God sending the plagues on the Egyptians; the parting of the Red Sea; the pillar of fire by night and the cloud by day; how He spoke to Moses on Mt. Sinai; the supernatural supply of manna daily; the water out of the rock; and how He brought them into the land that He had promised His people. It was the expressed desire of their heart to restore the

greatness of God to their present experience. They wanted
Him to do great things in their midst, and not just speak of
His greatness as a thing of the past.

5. God's Faithfulness

They prayed concerning the faithfulness of God (9:16–31).
He had been faithful to them even when they wanted to go
back to Egypt. He did not give up on them when they made
the golden calf. He continued to pour out His blessing upon
them and they reveled in it. Yet Israel was disobedient and
rebelled against God.

They entered the Promised Land, and during the time of
the Judges they entered a sin cycle. The sin cycle started when
Israel would turn away from the Lord God and allow sin to
enter into their lives. Then God would raise up a neighboring
nation to be their oppressor. After a period of oppression,
the people would repent and cry out to God for a deliverer.
God would raise up one such deliverer, a judge, and that
judge would deliver the people from the hand of the oppress-
ing nation. Soon, the cycle would start all over again as the
people would allow themselves to slip away from the Lord
God and sin would enter into their lives.

In all of His dealings with Israel, God did not give up on
them. Even when they were unfaithful to Him, He was faithful
to them.

6. Their Needs

They brought their needs before the Lord (9:32–35). They
recognized that they had been unfaithful to the Lord God
and yet He had been faithful to them through it all. They
asked that the Lord God would recognize their trouble and
give them first the grace they needed to make things right,
and then give them the continued strength to keep on living
right before Him. They also recognized that the situation they
were in was of their own doing as a nation.

7. Commitment

They made a new commitment to the Lord (9:36–38). It

was a demonstration that they meant business with God; they were through playing games with God. They would set forth six commitments to the Lord God and all sign their names to it. In this signed document, they would define their intentions. "That they were truly in earnest none can doubt," Ironside comments, "but the future would show once more, as the past so often had done, that man is not to be trusted, and that were God's covenant based on human faithfulness, instead of divine grace, all hope for man's lasting blessing would be vain."[9]

The redevelopment pastor must also be a man of prayer and he must lead his people in prayer. This means not only during prayer meetings and individual discipleship times, but also in board meetings when a particular problem is being faced, or when the congregation is facing a corporate decision. The people must know that he is a man of prayer, and this will motivate them to prayer. Remember, it was after Jesus had demonstrated His own prayer life that His disciples asked Him to teach them to pray like He prayed (Luke 11:1). People will believe that prayer is nothing more than mumbling words off into the atmosphere, unless they first see a genuine believer pray and see the results it brings.

Revival Produces New Life Convictions

Revival continues on as new life convictions are formed and principles of life are lived out from the Word of God (Nehemiah 10:1–39). To this end, Nehemiah and the people all signed their names to a document that set forth seven commitments which they vowed to follow in their new commitment to obey the Lord God:

1. Submission to Scripture

The first of these seven new commitments was that they would submit themselves to the authority of the Scriptures (10:28–29). They vowed to separate themselves "from the neighboring peoples for the sake of the Law of God, . . . to follow the Law of God, . . . and to obey carefully all the commands, regulations and decrees of the LORD our Lord."

With this renewed vow of commitment, they entered into a new relationship with the Lord God. In today's terms, it would mean they committed themselves to daily Bible study, Scripture memorization and meditation, and sitting under the preaching and teaching of the Word by others. It was not a passive, but an active commitment to the Scriptures.

2. Godly Marriages

Second, they committed themselves to God's highest purposes for their marriages (10:30). The nation of Israel was surrounded by heathen nations and it was so easy for the Jews to lose their national distinctiveness as the people of God (as evidenced by some of the priests who had intermarried in Nehemiah 7). "When morals of a nation are under stress," Swindoll notes, "the home is the first to suffer."[10] The people vowed that they would not let their sons and daughters marry those from the surrounding heathen nations. This would require committing themselves to the spiritual training of their children regarding: a. the importance of believing friends and marriage partners; b. the consequences of violating this scriptural principle.

3. Keeping the Sabbath

Third, they committed themselves to a recognition of the Lord's day and the observance of it (10:31). They would restrict secular activities in order to make the day holy unto the Lord God and they also would observe the forgiveness of debts owed them at the Sabbath year. There can be no genuine commitment to worshiping the Lord unless there is also an accompanying commitment to honor Him by observing His day.

4. Temple Offerings

Fourth, they committed themselves to the bringing in of the temple offerings (10:32-33). Previously, in Exodus 30:11-16, the Lord had told Moses to take up a similar offering for the service of the tabernacle. But that was a one-time offering taken at the same time as when Moses took the census. Here, the people made a different type of pledge for the same type of offering. It was a smaller offering, but it was to be given annually. The Exodus offering was to be half a shekel, whereas the Nehemiah offering was to be a third of a shekel. God's people cannot really say that they have committed their souls to Him for all eternity, if they are not willing to commit their money to Him in the present. It comes down to whether we trust the Lord or just say we do, and it is our commitment to bringing in the offerings in worship of the Lord that will tell the difference.

In times previous, Cyrus, Darius and Artaxerxes had given money for rebuilding the temple, but the people knew that the Lord's work was not to be carried on by such grants from heathen nations. God's work is to be supported by God's people and they vowed to take up that responsibility.

5. Doing the Chores

Fifth, they committed themselves to performing the temple service once again (Nehemiah 10:34–36). Lots were cast to choose those who would bring in the wood, so that there could be fire on the altar at all times as the law prescribed. In their commentary, C.F. Keil and F. Delitzsch explain:

> The Law gave no directions concerning the procuring of the wood; yet the rulers of the people must at all the events, have always provided for the regular delivery of the necessary quantity. Nehemiah now gives orders which make this matter the business of the congregation, and the several houses have successively to furnish a contribution, in the order decided by casting lots."[11]

This is just like paying the utility bills at the church. It is a necessary part of the overall ministry, but it is not considered too spiritual a function. Somebody has to bring in the firewood for the altar fires, and offerings have to be used to pay utility bills. It is all part of the ministry.

6. Firstfruits

Sixth, they pledged to bring in their firstfruit offerings to the Lord each year, firstfruits of all their crops, cattle, sons, flocks, etc. All of this was to enhance the service of the temple so that the ministries could be carried out effectively. It also was an indication that they recognized that the Lord was the real owner of their possessions and their livelihood and they were stewards, not owners.

7. Supporting the Ministry

Seventh, the people of Jerusalem pledged themselves to bring in support for the temple and to support those who ministered in it (10:37–39). These forms of support were in the firstfruit offerings, tithes of their harvests and tithes of their money. The temple had once again become the center of their lives. Here again, the use of one's money will reveal where his or her heart really lies (Matthew 7:21). If a person genuinely loves the Lord, he or she will support His work and His messengers.

Here again, the people of the declining ministry need to see that their pastor is a man whose life is governed by convictions, and that these convictions are based squarely upon the Word of God. The redevelopment pastor must also seek in his preaching and teaching ministry to dwell upon the practical applications of the passage of Scripture being presented. The people need something practical that they can put a handle on and carry back to their homes, schools and workplaces. God's people need to make life commitments based upon the Word of God. And their pastor must lead them to make these commitments.

Chapter 15

A Place for Everyone to Serve

[11:1–36]

Nehemiah then faced a new situation in his ministry. The walls had been rebuilt, faithful men had been appointed to positions of leadership, revival had come through a time of reading of the Word and prayer, new commitments had been entered into by the signing of a document and there had been a celebration of the Feast of Tabernacles. But after the celebration had been completed and Jerusalem was empty, all the people returned to their homes, leaving the city in a restored, but empty condition. "Jerusalem was not the most popular place to live; the masses of people evidently preferred to reside elsewhere," Campbell explains. "In the capital, the cost of living was no doubt higher, there was a housing shortage, jobs were not plentiful, and personal safety could not be guaranteed."[1] If Jerusalem was to be the thriving city it once was, Nehemiah had to find some way to repopulate the city.

The Scriptures say in Nehemiah 7:4, "Now the city was large and spacious, but there were few people in it, and the houses had not yet been rebuilt." Later, in Nehemiah 11:1, the Scriptures go on to say that the leaders of the people settled in Jerusalem. When Nehemiah spoke to the ones whom he had appointed to positions of leadership in Nehemiah 7, he must have told them that he wanted them to live in Jerusalem. Now Nehemiah had to get the common people to move to Jerusalem.

What could Nehemiah possibly offer them that would motivate them to leave the homes they had established in the country and villages surrounding Jerusalem and begin life all over again? As the ruling official, the governor, Nehemiah could just have ordered the people to move and that would have settled the issue. Albert Barnes states that this would fit the historical period. "Artificial enlargements of capitals by forcible transfers of population to them, were not unusual in ancient times."[2] But the Scriptures record that was not the method of repopulating Jerusalem that Nehemiah chose.

The method of transferring the people to Jerusalem was that of casting lots. Casting lots was not unusual to determine the will of God in Israel (Numbers 26:55–56; Joshua 18:10; 1 Samuel 14:41; 1 Chronicles 24:5, 25:8; Esther 3:7; Proverbs 16:33; et al).

It is not said who came up with the idea of casting lots or of how the figure of one in 10 was arrived at, but that was the outcome of the decision. There was a dual aspect of casting lots. Those who were chosen did not rebel against the aspect of moving to Jerusalem, but they voluntarily left their homes, knowing that it was the will of God for their lives that they should go.

After those who had been chosen took up their new residences in Jerusalem, an insight into the reason why God selected those to relocate becomes clear. Every one of the people had a particular function to perform. Nehemiah, chapter 11, lists these responsibilities as:

1. those who performed the work of the temple (v. 12);
2. mighty men of valor (v. 14, KJV);
3. leaders of the Levites who were in charge of the work outside of the house of God (v. 16);
4. prayer warriors (v. 17);
5. those who kept watch at the gates (v. 19);

6. those who were singers for the services in the temple (v. 22);
7. one who was the liaison between the people and the king concerning matters that related to the people (v. 24).

Everyone was selected by the Lord God, through the process of casting lots, because of their individual skills for service in the renewed Jerusalem. They were to be more than just people to fill the city; they were to give their abilities in service to the Lord God in His city, Jerusalem.

Though the New Testament does not indicate we should carry on the practice of casting lots, there is a principle here for the redevelopment pastor to use. In Philippians 4:19 the Bible promises, "And my God will meet all your needs according to his glorious riches in Christ Jesus." This applies equally to individual believers as it does to corporate believers. When a redevelopment pastor needs someone to serve in a ministry capacity in the church, he needs to pray that the Lord would supply someone with those gifts to fill the need that exists. I have prayed for a piano player when the church had none to play for our services. I have also prayed for Sunday school teachers when we had a class but no teacher. I have prayed for those with financial means when the church had no finances to carry on the ministry. Jerusalem was God's city and Nehemiah looked to Him to populate the city and supply people for ministry needs. And the redevelopment pastor can ask the Lord to do the same for His church.

It Takes All Kinds

The first group of people selected for a specific task did the work in the temple. Their list of duties probably included the care of the interior building and furniture. They were to make sure that everything physically necessary for the temple worship was ready.

Those who were selected to be the mighty men of valor were charged with the defense of the city. Israel, and

Jerusalem in particular, was held in disgust by the surrounding nations. In the past these nations had seized every opportunity to take advantage of Jerusalem's broken down condition and would not be pleased to have the city protected from their plundering. So some of the Israelite men were charged with the defense.

It is not certain what those who were selected to do the work outside the temple actually did. As it is written here, it can mean one of two things. It could "refer to the outside appearance of the temple," F. Charles Fensham suggests. "Another possibility is that this outside work entails the collecting of the tithes, the temple taxes."[3]

The fourth in the list of responsibilities given to the people was for a leader in the ministry of prayer. Nehemiah knew that if the work of the Lord in Jerusalem was to continue on and be blessed of God, prayer had to be undergirding it all. Mattaniah was selected to fulfill this function because of his prayer life. Every man of God needs a Mattaniah to hold both him and the work God has called him to before the Lord in earnest prayer.

Fifth, the gatekeepers saw that the gates were kept in good repair and were opened every morning, except the Sabbath, and closed every evening. Derek Kidner has the following to say about the gatekeepers:

> The duties of these gatekeeper families are explained more fully in 1 Chronicles 9:17–27, where it appears that the security of the temple area was their hereditary charge, and that their number was supplemented by non-resident kinsmen who came in from their villages for a week's duty at a time. The temple needed a strong guard on account of both its treasures and its sacredness.[4]

The next group of servants were the singers. Music is an integral part of praising and worshiping the Lord God, and the singers were chosen to use their voices to praise the Lord and to lead others musically in His worship.

Finally, there was one appointed to be the king's representative, or liaison officer, in all matters concerning the people. This position was one of protocol and would help ensure an absence of conflict between the civil administration of a Persian king and the religious life of the Jewish people. Nehemiah knew that people would respond to civil rule much more readily if they knew their religious liberties were being protected. Barber points out the political climate:

> In the absence of a king in Judah, and God's rule over his people through a local (theocratic) representative, a form of democracy prevails. It is a democracy established upon a strong religious foundation. Normatively there is a justice, equity, and equality. Structurally there is a distribution of power with the people sharing in the affairs of their community. Behaviorally there is an absence of conflict. All of this finds its origin in the relationship of the people to the Lord and their desire to do his will.[5]

Since the method of selection by which families were chosen to relocate in Jerusalem was the sovereign desire of God, we need to be careful not to think less of those who were not chosen. In the same way that the Lord God chose families to live in Jerusalem, we can also say that He chose the rest to continue living where they were. In Nehemiah 11:3, we read how some were left to stay in the areas outside the city. Campbell gives an overview of the situation:

> There were no second-class citizens. It was essential that the majority of the population live outside Jerusalem in rural towns and villages, farming the land and raising animals for food and sacrifice. Not all could live in the city made holy by the temple and the presence of the Lord. Some, in the will of God had to live elsewhere and they too were honored servants of God.[6]

For the redevelopment pastor, this chapter demonstrates two very important truths in helping him to turn a declining ministry into a growing one:

1. He must seek to have a core group of people who know it is God's will for them to be there.
2. Those that come to be a part of the new work must be *workers*, not merely pew warmers.

Generally speaking, people attend a particular church either for what the church can offer them or for what they can offer the church. The redevelopment pastor must not get discouraged when visitors come to his church and seldom return. Not many people have the vision nor the heart for the Lord to be involved in a new, growing work. The redevelopment pastor needs to seek the Lord in prayer for this second group. If you need a piano player, pray for one. If you need a Sunday school teacher, pray for the Lord to send one to you. Whatever the ministry personnel needs may be, the redevelopment pastor can pray for the Lord of the harvest to send them to him (Luke 10:2; Philippians 4:19). A declining ministry is seldom turned into a growing one simply because there has been a pastoral change. There needs to be an infusion of "new blood" into the life of the church and that will only come as the Lord sends those who are seeking where they can be used of the Lord for His service in a local ministry. There are few greater encouragements to a redevelopment pastor than when new people come with an attitude to be his co-workers in the new ministry under his leadership.

Just as the redevelopment pastor needs to pray that the Lord will send him workers for the ministry, he needs to pray that the Lord will keep away those for whom it is not His will to be there. It is a freeing realization for the redevelopment pastor to understand that he cannot minister to everyone in the particular work in which he is engaged. He must also pray that the Lord God would protect both him and the work from those who would tear it down rather than help build it up.

Six Guiding Principles

Every pastor, and especially a redevelopment pastor, needs to find a place of service for everyone who comes to be a part of the growing ministry. In the exercise of the various spiritual gifts within the ministry, the pastors need to bear in mind at least six guiding principles. These guidelines are not meant to be exhaustive on the subject of spiritual gifts, but to emphasize some basic understandings.

1. Everyone Has at Least One

Every believer has at least one spiritual gift with which to serve the Lord (1 Peter 4:10; 1 Corinthians 12:7, 11), and some may have more than one. First Corinthians 12:7 tells us that spiritual gifts are not for a few elite people. In addition, two Christians may have the same gift, but differ in their capacity for service. Whatever the gift and whatever the capacity for ministry, God intends every Christian to be active in the service for which he has been gifted.

2. The Gifts Are for Service

Spiritual gifts are given for service to the body of Christ (1 Peter 4:10; Ephesians 4:12; 1 Corinthians 12:7). Spiritual gifts are tools to be used and not toys to be played with. They are given for the sole purpose of serving the Body of Christ by edification and evangelization. They are not meant to bring glory to the Christian; they are only the instrument through which the Lord Jesus Christ ministers to His church and reaches a lost world with the gospel of salvation.

3. Everyone Should Serve

Each member should have an opportunity to use his gift(s) interdependently with others (Romans 12:4-6; Ephesians 4:16; 1 Peter 4:10). No one person has all the gifts. Everyone within the ministry has at least one of the spiritual gifts and is therefore gifted to be used in a particular ministry within the church. So within the church there are several people all serving the Lord in the way He designed them to serve, making each one dependent upon the other for ministry in the church as a whole. It is the responsibility of the pastor to make sure that every individual in the ministry has ample training to perfect his spiritual gift so that he can be able to carry out his ministry.

4. Love Is the Key

The motivation behind the exercise of a spiritual gift is love (1 Corinthians 12:31–13:13). It is not a coincidence that the love chapter of the Bible, First Corinthians 13, falls between two chapters dealing with spiritual gifts. Love for the Lord Jesus Christ and love for others is to be the motivation behind the operation of all spiritual gifts. Otherwise their employment is merely mechanical and void of any practical, spiritual ministry that touches people's lives.

5. Everyone Is Necessary

Each member with his gift(s) is necessary to the whole ministry. Therefore if any member is not active in the ministry, the ministry as a whole is weakened (1 Corinthians 12:14–26). Fred Fisher explains the concept very well:

> Without stating his application in so many words, Paul suggested several points of comparison between the physical body and the congregation: (1) Each is an organism composed of many parts; (2) Each body is complete only when the various parts perform their diverse functions; (3) In a body each member is dependent on every other member; (4) Discord destroys the reality of a body in each case.[7]

The redevelopment pastor needs to remind the people of the growing church that they each have something uniquely vital to offer to the overall ministry and challenge them to be faithful in carrying out the ministry the Lord has given them.

6. The Lord Will Provide

The Holy Spirit will give all the gifts that are necessary to carry out the work of the Lord in a given area (1 Corinthians

12:7; Ephesians 4:12–16). In a small ministry (such as a declining ministry) there is always a great sense of burden for the redevelopment pastor to start new ministries to meet the needs of his own congregation. The tendency for him to fulfill the leadership in that ministry often means soon he is involved in so many various functions within the church that he is lacking effectiveness in all of them. If a ministry burden falls upon a pastor, he should next give himself to prayer as to who will carry out this ministry. And if it is genuinely from the Lord, he will supply someone to take the leadership for the particular ministry (Philippians 4:19). The Lord will either send someone new who has those particular skills and gifts, or he will raise up someone from within the group who was previously uninvolved.

Like Nehemiah in Jerusalem, the redevelopment pastor must "repopulate" the ministry with those whom the Lord sends and then seek to find a place of ministry for everyone in which they can serve the Lord Jesus.

Chapter 16

The Service of Rededication

[12:1–47]

At some point in the redevelopment pastor's work with the declining ministry, he will notice a change for the good taking place. He will notice the work developing into a growing work.

The physical facilities will have been repaired. During this time of repair, the redevelopment pastor will have observed who the real workers in the ministry actually are. Also during this time, he will have helped the people work through some of their personal problems. He will have warded off attempts from the enemy to halt the new work that is going on in the declining ministry during transition. Faithful men will be in positions of leadership and there will be a new seriousness about the things of God. The people will be supporting the work of the Lord not only with their presence, but with their finances as well. In addition, the people will have a new interest in the Word of God and in prayer that results in a renewed conviction to live by the Scriptures. A core group will begin to form from new people whom the Lord has sent to the ministry.

It will be at this point that the redevelopment pastor should consider having a service of rededication of the people and the facilities—a celebration of a renewed focus on the purposes of God for their lives.

People need this type of service as a focal point, to emphasize that the work has taken on a new, upward direction. This is exactly what Nehemiah did in Jerusalem when he began to sense that the work had made a transition from decline to growth—for the glory of the Lord God. This service of rededication that Nehemiah led the people through is described for us in chapter 12 of Nehemiah. When did this service take place? Campbell attempts to answer that question:

> Since no date is given for the dedication, various intervals after the completion of the walls have been proposed. Some even suggest it took place 12 years later and was the occasion of Nehemiah's return from Persia for his second term as governor. But among the ancient Hebrews, dedication rites were considered the final act of building (see Deuteronomy 20:5) and it is only natural to assume the ceremony took place soon after the walls were rebuilt.[1]

This service of rededication is a formal point at which people may look back to lessons learned regarding past failures of the work in a noncondemning way, but from which they also purpose to strike out on a new course. There must be an examination as to why the ministry became a declining ministry, in order to not inadvertently repeat the problems in the future.

An "Order of Service" for the Rededication

Nehemiah's service of rededication had seven parts:

1. Recognition

First, there was a recognition of those who had a part in bringing about the turnaround for this new beginning (Nehemiah 12:1-26). This list was a memorial to those who had left their homes in Babylon and had returned to Jerusalem. But it was more than that; it was a listing of those people who had worked hard and long to reestablish God's testimony in His city once again. As people would read Nehemiah's book in the years that followed, the names of these people would become examples to all because of their diligence and labors for the Lord God.

Beginning with Zerubbabel, Nehemiah lists the priests and Levites right up to his own time. These are the ones who returned from the Babylonian captivity with the goal of rebuilding the city. This list of names is divided up into three areas: (1) the priests and Levites of Zerubbabel's return (12:1–9), (2) postexilic high priests (12:10–11) and (3) priests and Levites after Zerubbabel and Jeshua (12:12–26).

2. Music

Second, there was singing and musical praise and joy by the Levites from the plain country round about Jerusalem, and from the villages of Netophathi, Beth Gilgal, Geba and Azmaveth (12:27–29). "Their joy that day in the dedication of the wall was the joy of the Lord. A great deal of material splendor that marked former years had gone, but surely now there could not be a greater glory in their devotion to the will of God and surrender for his purpose."[2] And since music plays such a large part of praise to the Lord, it was only right that the singers be summoned to take part in the service.

3. Consecration

As the service of dedication got underway, the next item on the program was that of a time of personal consecration (12:30). A new beginning called for a new cleansing. Further, personal holiness was the basis for all the workings of the priests in service to the Lord God. Once previously, under King Hezekiah, Jerusalem was called to a time of corporate cleansing (2 Chronicles 29:17–24). The priests and the Levites of Nehemiah's day most likely began their cleansing with the temple and then brought in the necessary offerings for all of the people; just as their fathers had done in Hezekiah's day. This is the basis of the New Testament principle that when cleansing or judgment is to begin, it "must begin with the family of God" (1 Peter 4:17).

4. Processional

Following the time of consecration was the processional of the choirs (Nehemiah 12:31–39). Nehemiah divided the people up into two groups; Nehemiah led one group and Ezra led the other group. The two groups walked through Jerusalem to the top of the walls and circled the city, meeting near the temple for the dedication service.

We can safely assume what activities took place as they marched around the top of the wall. Along with the choirs were musicians who marched and played their instruments to accompany the singers. And the songs that they sang were songs of God's faithfulness in helping them to rebuild the walls and the city and in protecting them throughout it all. There were also probably musical themes of the glory of God as He once had dwelt in Jerusalem. This rededication service had a sight and a sound that would raise their hearts in worship of the Lord God for all that He had done through them.

5. Dedication

Fifth, there was a service of dedication anew unto the Lord (12:40–42). Nehemiah's mind must have been flooded with memories ranging from that first day in the palace when he heard the initial report of the condition of the people and of Jerusalem, to his meeting with the king and the trip to Jersualem, to the months of praying, planning and working through all the internal and external problems he encountered in the work.

And now, the wall was finished, the people were revived. It was a time for all to praise the Lord God for what He had done for them. It was also a time for the people to rejoice in the Lord as well for all His goodness toward them. As the songs of dedication were sung, they all praised the Lord for what He had done and voiced their commitment and dependence upon Him who was their help and strength.

6. Offering

Sixth, as an overflow of the peoples' sacrifices of praise to the Lord, offerings for His work were given (12:43). Today, when people give of their possessions to the Lord, this shows that they are really thankful to the Lord for a particular work in their lives. It has been said that the last area of man's being to be conquered is his wallet. When people give of their money, it is a true indication that Jesus is Lord of the other areas of their life as well.

7. Commitment

Finally, there was an onward commitment to worship (12:44–47). Men were appointed to collect the tithes from the people, and those who served in the temple were to be supported by these finances. When God's people appreciate the work of their spiritual leaders, they want to give their tithes and offerings unto the Lord for the needs of God's work and for the needs of their leaders.

The service of rededication that the redevelopment pastor plans should also contain these same features which Nehemiah included in his service. There should be the involvement of the people who helped rebuild the facility, singing, a time of personal cleansing and commitment to the ongoing work of the Lord. The service should conclude with an offering for the work of the Lord. This type of service will become a milestone in the time to come, a time when the people look back to when the new work began.

Having conducted a rededication service and having seen the difference it makes, I would encourage redevelopment pastors to hold such a service and to take the lead in it. It will prove to be a time which the people look back on as a turnaround in the life of their church, a time when hope and vision became guiding principles, rather than an attitude of survival.

Chapter 17

The Problem of Leaving Too Soon

[13:1–31]

In the process of turning a ministry from decline to growth, the redevelopment pastor must keep two things in mind. First, the biblical convictions of the leader often set the pace for the whole congregation; second, the ministry takes on characteristics that reflect those convictions. Since one of the major reasons a ministry declines is a lack of biblical convictions, the redevelopment pastor should be firm in what he believes.

As his ministry begins to unfold, he naturally teaches from his biblical perspective and the people take their cue from that. But deep biblical convictions take a lot of time and testing to develop before the people are able to stand on their own. If a pastor leaves that particular ministry too soon, the work may revert back to the condition it was in prior to his coming. If the peoples' convictions are in the process of being formed and the pastor leaves too soon, it will take even more time than it would otherwise for their convictions as a body of believers to become solidified. The redevelopment pastor can nullify all his hard work by leaving that ministry too soon.

Often the elements that formerly brought the work into spiritual decay are still present—either just outside the door or lying dormantly within. If, for instance, the ministry began to decline because of carnal leadership on the governing board and a heavy turnover factor in the pastoral leadership (which is not unusual for declining ministries), those carnal leaders may be content to "lie low" for a while, waiting for the pastor to leave so they can get back in the driver's seat again. So there can be a sense in the redevelopment pastor's mind that things are really different, when in actuality they are not. The opposition is only waiting until he exits like others before him. They may even go to another church and wait on the outside until the pastor leaves. Either way, if the redevelopment pastor leaves too soon, these carnal people, who want to run the ministry the way they see fit (as opposed to following scriptural guidelines), lie waiting for their chance to take over again as soon as the pastor leaves.

Leaving too soon is very common—in fact, even a leader as outstanding as Nehemiah made that mistake. In chapter 13 we see the results of his premature departure. Nehamiah was able to return and straighten out the problems, but a redevelopment pastor seldom has that opportunity; he must recognize and deal with the temptation to make a hasty exit.

Why Do They Leave So Soon?

Why do redevelopment pastors leave the work so soon— sometimes just as it's starting to succeed? I have observed four reasons why this takes place:

1. He Needs a Break!

First is the need for relief from the difficult work that he has just completed. The redevelopment pastor faces tremendous pressures that hardly anyone else can relate to other than another redevelopment pastor. There are spiritual pressures from being in the forefront of the spiritual battle. The devil simply does not want a declining ministry to become a growing ministry and he will stop at nothing to accomplish his goals. As the battle wears on, the redevelopment pastor often wears down. When the battle first gives any hint that it is over, the redevelopment pastor feels the need to move on to another place where the grass is greener and where he can heal his battle scars.

2. He Needs the Money!

Second, there is the matter of the financial pressures of ministering in a declining ministry. The redevelopment pastor, no matter what his education or experience may be, often receives a much smaller salary than he is worthy of receiving. When the ministry begins to grow again and those in that ministry do not immediately seek to raise his salary, he will be tempted to move on to another ministry where appreciation from the congregation is expressed with a greater sensitivity to his financial needs.

3. He Needs a Challenge!

Third, he might feel the need for a new challenge after the present work is completed. There is personal exhilaration involved in taking a declining ministry and seeing it grow under the guiding hand of the Lord God. And some men thrive on that type of challenge so much that they fail to carry out the transition until it is genuinely completed. These pastors need to come to terms with the reality that it is just as important to leave only under the call of God, as it was to come under the call of God.

4. He Can't Switch Gears!

Fourth, he has a fear of failure in carrying on the work now that it has been changed from a declining ministry to a growing ministry. In a declining ministry, almost all the decisions are made by the redevelopment pastor. But in a growing ministry, the spiritual leadership is shared with other faithful men—and this change of operational procedure sometimes does not set well with the redevelopment pastor. He is used to making all the decisions and doing things in his own manner. That is not all bad, since it was his leadership that brought the change in the ministry. But leadership must change to meet the needs of the ones it seeks to lead. Redevelopment pastors who cannot make personal adjustments in their leadership style often leave their work before it is genuinely finished.

Though there are several other pressures that the redevelopment pastor comes under in the process of turning a declining ministry into a growing one, these seem to be the most pressing issues for a pastor to leave too soon.

Redevelopment pastors and their church governing boards must recognize this danger and make alternatives available to the pastor. Soon after the service of rededication (no later than four months), the governing board should give their pastor a two-to-four-week paid leave of absence which is not to be counted toward his regular vacation time. In addition, it would be good to have a special love offering to give to him as well, so he can take his wife and family on an extended get-away. Congregations who recognize the heavy toll a declining ministry takes on their pastor and family will gladly see the need for giving him a needed time away. The alternative is that he will be tempted to leave and they will have to start over with someone new.

It Should Have Ended Here!

It would have been good for the book of Nehemiah to have ended with chapter 12 and the service of dedication, but it did not. Sometime after the service of dedication, Nehemiah left Jerusalem to return to the palace in Susa. He told King Artaxerxes that he would be back in a certain time and he left in order to keep his word. We are not told how long Nehemiah was in Susa; but at some point while he was there he heard of new breakdowns in Jerusalem's leadership and he asked to return there where he stayed for a total of 12 years of service.

Problem #1—An Enemy in Power

In 13:4–9, the first problem that Nehemiah faced was that, in his absence, Tobiah was allowed to set up a room within the temple. Tobiah, who had been one of those who tried to halt the rebuilding work of both the wall and the people of God (2:10), was now living and working from within the very temple he had hoped to destroy. How or why he was allowed to come in we do not know. We do know that Tobiah was related to Eliashib, probably through marriage of a daughter of Eliashib's. From within the temple of God, Tobiah was allowed to set up his central headquarters to work evil in the midst of the people of God.

Upon his return, Nehemiah threw out Tobiah's furniture and ordered the temple cleansed. Nehemiah knew that what Tobiah had been allowed to do was evil and had to be dealt with immediately and without mercy. It is significant that Eliashib evidently stood by as Nehemiah proceeded to throw Tobiah out of the temple. He did nothing to stop Nehemiah's work. It can presumably be held that Eliashib was a man who had no real convictions of his own toward the work of God; he could be swayed one way or the other in the presence of a man of convictions.

Problem #2—Lack of Support

The next problem that Nehemiah had to deal with was lack of support for those who worked in the service of the temple (13:10–14). For whatever reason, the people quit giving their tithes and offerings sometime after Nehemiah left to go back to the palace. Prompting God's people to withhold the Lord's tithe money is one of the most common tactics of the devil. He knows that if he can get the people to quit supporting the work that one of two things will happen: the spiritual leaders will either leave or be forced to supplement their income with a second job. Either way the enemy wins. If the spiritual leader leaves due to lack of financial support, the devil has won outright. If the spiritual leader is forced to take outside employment, his energies will be spread so thin that any eternal damage he might inflict upon Satan's kingdom is negligible.

In this case, the Levites had moved out to do farming in order to support themselves. Nehemiah spoke to the rulers (13:11) concerning this act of disobedience to the Scriptures and then set about to collect the tithes which were due the Lord.

When God's people refuse to worship Him with their tithes

and offerings, three things happen:

1. God sends a "devourer" to eat up the paycheck with unexpected expenses;
2. God is not able to bless His people as He would like to do;
3. the needs of the work of the Lord are not met.

In this case, the Levites and the singers were neglected (Malachi 3:10–11). Finances are rarely a problem in a church, but they are almost always a symptom of a problem. When there is a need in one of those three areas—unusual extra expenses, church needs going unmet, evident lack of blessing—the first question the pastor should ask is "Are you tithing your income to the Lord?" More often than not the answer will be "No."

Nehemiah ends his description of what he did to remedy this situation with a record of the brief prayer that he offered up to the Lord God regarding his efforts (Nehemiah 13:14). He had worked long and hard in order to establish once again the testimony of the Lord God in Jerusalem and Nehemiah requested of the Lord God that his effort would not be wiped out. "Being himself one who trusted the Lord, Nehemiah humbly asked that the work that he did might come under remembrance before God," Alan Redpath comments. "To serve Him here for a reward is not our motive, but it is a tremendous strength in the battle to know that one day there is a 'well done' awaiting us if we have been faithful to him."[1]

Further, he asked that he be remembered for the work of the Lord that he had done. There are two ways in which the Lord God answered this prayer. First, when people who know their Bibles hear his name, they immediately think of the great work that Nehemiah did in the restoration of God's people and God's city. But more than that, God Himself will remember Nehemiah's efforts and will reward him one day in heaven, when the saints of Israel are resurrected. The work that God's people do for Him now may or may not gain the attention of the world in general, but we can be sure that God sees and remembers and will one day give the reward.

Problem #3—Lack of Obedience

A third wrong that Nehemiah saw in Jerusalem upon his return was lack of obedience to the Lord in the Sabbath observance (13:15-22). Just as today in the observance of Sunday as the "Lord's day," so it was with the observance of the Jewish Sabbath. It is one of the indications of whom a person really worships. Today, some come to Sunday morning worship service more out of duty than out of a desire to worship corporately, and then go on to spend the "Lord's day" with family or friends. Their god is not the God, but the god of family, friends or leisure activities. Some open their places of business on the Lord's day, and their god is money. If the Lord's day is the Lord's day, then it ought to be given to Him and His worship and not to anyone or anything else.

Nehemiah saw this breaking of the Sabbath as a serious matter—it was disobedience to the revealed Word of God. He knew that the people could not expect to live under God's blessing if they continued to disobey what He had already said to them. Nehemiah commanded that the gates be shut and none of the merchants be allowed inside to do their business on the Sabbath again. And when they continued to loiter around the outside of the wall, he threatened them to leave or else he would fight them all by himself. And he probably would have won—as he had demonstrated in verse 25, when he took on all the fathers of the city who had let their sons and daughters marry foreigners.

For the second time in this chapter, Nehemiah ends his dealings with a problem by praying for God's remembrance. It is interesting that, even in the heat of battle when Nehemiah's adrenalin was flowing in abundance, he turned to the Lord God in prayer as the source of his life. Nehemiah never forgot that he was in the very presence of God, or that he was His servant doing His will. "Whether this aggressive and dedicated leader was dealing with enemies foreign or domestic, whether he was involved in political, social, or religious issues," Campbell observes, "fellowship with God in prayer was always top priority."[2]

Problem #4—Divided Hearts

Last, Nehemiah discovered that mixed marriages were being consummated in Jerusalem in disobedience to the will of God (13:23–31). In Deuteronomy 23:3, the Lord God had specifically forbidden His people from allowing Ammonites or Moabites to ever enter the congregation of Israel. When he returned, Nehemiah saw that they had disobeyed the Lord God and taken wives of the very people which God had forbidden them to even allow into their midst.

What a sight it must have been as Nehemiah set out to remedy the situation. Nehemiah began yelling at them, some he began beating. From others he plucked out their hair. He made them swear that they would not allow this practice to go on anymore. One of the grandsons of Eliashib had married a daughter of Sanballat. When Nehemiah saw and heard what he had done, he physically ran the grandson out of town. He reminded all the people that intermarriages divided Solomon's heart. And Solomon's divided heart led to a divided kingdom and later to the downfall of both parts. Nehemiah wanted them to know the long range consequences of marrying a non-believer. "No doubt some would speak of his ways as hard and bitter," H.A. Ironside comments, "but sin is hard and bitter; persistency in it often requires severe measures to put things right."[3] Nehemiah took swift, violent action against those who disobeyed the Lord God because he knew the great danger such actions would produce in the years to come if not dealt with. Anything less would indicate acceptance of the sin.

Nehemiah was always aware of the presence of the Lord God and often talked with Him in prayer. Again, Nehemiah closed out his dealings with mixed marriages by praying to the Lord God for His remembrance. His whole life was energized by the fact that he was a servant of the Lord God acting in His behalf and in His presence.

Nehemiah's book provides us with a manual for all who are in positions of spiritual leadership, and especially for all redevelopment pastors who feel the call of God on their life to change a declining ministry into a growing one. Just as Nehemiah prayed that God would remember him, I am praying that you will remember God as you rebuild the ministry to which He has called you.

FOOTNOTES

Chapter 1

1. Figures taken from graphs in an article, "Worship Attendance for U. S. Churches," in Issue #21 (no date) of the *Winn Arn Church Growth Report,* page 1; published by Church Growth, Incorporated, 1921 South Myrtle Avenue, Monrovia, California 91016.

2. Ibid.

Chapter 3

1. Chart was adapted from: Cyril J. Barber, *Nehemiah and the Dynamics of Effective Leadership* (Neptune, NJ: Loizeaux Brothers 1978), p. 21.

2. Charles R. Swindoll, *Hand Me Another Brick* (Nashville: Thomas Nelson Inc. 1978), p. 139.

3. These benefits of fasting are summarized from an unpublished handout given to the author while he was a student at Columbia Bible College, Columbia, SC.

4. John R. Rice, *Prayer: Asking and Receiving* (Wheaton, IL: Sword of the Lord Publishers 1952), p. 220.

5. Ronald A. Ward, *Commentary on 1 & 2 Timothy & Titus* (Waco, TX: Word Publishing 1976), p. 58.

6. Adam Clarke, *Clarke's Commentary on the Old and New Testaments* (New York: Lane & Scott 1851), Vol II, p. 764.

7. Ibid. pp. 764–765.

Chapter 4

1. James Orr, gen. ed., *The International Standard Bible Encyclopedia* (Grand Rapids, MI: William B. Eerdmans Publishing Co. 1939), Vol. II, p. 766.

2. Robert Jamieson, A.R. Fausset and David Brown, *A Commentary on the Old and New Testaments* (Grand Rapids, MI: Zondervan, n.d.), Vol. I, Part II, p. 607.

3. Richard Seume, *Nehemiah: God's Builder* (Chicago: Moody Press 1978), p. 27.

4. J. Oswald Sanders, *Spiritual Leadership* (Chicago: Moody Press 1967), p. 120.

5. Ted W. Engstrom, *The Making of a Christian Leader* (Grand Rapids, MI: Zondervan Publishing Company 1976), p. 170.

Chapter 5

1. R. Laird Harris, Gleason L. Archer, Jr., and Bruce K. Waltke, *Theological Wordbook of the Old Testament* (Chicago: Moody Press 1981), Vol. II, p. 415.

2. W. J. Conybeare and J. S. Howson, *The Life and Epistles of St. Paul* (Grand Rapids, MI: William B. Eerdmans Publishing Co. 1980, 16th printing) p. 50.

3. Jay E. Adams, *The Pastoral Life* (Grand Rapids, MI: Baker Book House 1975) pp. 33–34.

Chapter 6

1. In *The Making of a Christian Leader*, Ted Engstrom describes the styles of leadership in five categories:
(1) laissez-faire,
(2) democratic-participative,
(3) manipulative-inspirational,
(4) benevolent-autocratic, and
(5) autocratic-bureaucratic.

In *So You Want to Be a Leader!* (Camp Hill, PA: Christian
Publications, Inc.), Kenneth O. Gangel describes the styles of
leadership in three categories: (1) autocratic, (2) free-rein,
and (3) participatory.

2. William Barclay, *The Gospel of Matthew* (Philadelphia: The
Westminster Press 1975), Vol. II, pp. 233–234.

Chapter 7

1. John C. Thiessen, *Pastoring the Smaller Church* (Grand
Rapids, MI: Zonderan Publishing House 1973), p. 19.

2. Ibid, p. 18.

Chapter 8

1. Gene A. Getz, *Nehemiah: A Man of Prayer and Persistence*
(Ventura, CA: Regal Books 1981), pp. 29–30.

2. Sanders, p. 82.

3. Getz, p. 30.

4. Cyril J. Barber, *Nehemiah and the Dynamics of Effective
Leadership* (Neptune, NJ: Loizeaux Brothers 1978), p. 31.

Chapter 9

1. Getz, p. 35.

2. Matthew Henry, *Matthew Henry's Commentary on the Whole
Bible* (McLean, VA: MacDonald Publishing Company n.d.),
Vol. II, p. 1073.

3. Engstrom, p. 201.

4. Ibid. p. 201.

Chapter 10

1. Kenneth O. Gangel, *Competent to Lead* (Chicago: Moody
Press 1974), pp. 84–85.

2. Swindoll, p. 83.

3. Ibid. p. 64.

4. Barber, p. 42.

5. Ibid. p. 42.

Chapter 11

1. Swindoll, p. 67.

2. Donald K. Campbell, *Nehemiah: Man in Charge* (Wheaton, IL: Victor Books 1979), p. 36.

3. Swindoll, p. 78.

4. Campbell, p. 54.

5. F. Charles Fensham, *The Books of Ezra and Nehemiah* (Grand Rapids, MI: Wm. B. Eerdmans Publishing Company 1983), pp. 200–201.

6. Barber, p. 42.

Chapter 12

1. James Allen Sparks, *Potshots at the Preacher* (Nashville: Abingdon 1977), pp. 20–30 (condensed).

2. Barber, p. 85.

3. Dwight L. Carlson, *Overcoming Hurts & Anger* (Eugene, OR: Harvest House Publishers 1981), p. 92.

4. Seume, p. 70.

Chapter 13

1. Campbell, p. 62.

2. Ron Jenson and Jim Stevens, *Dynamics of Church Growth* (Grand Rapids, MI: Baker Book House 1981), pp. 111–112.

3. Kenneth O. Gangel, *So You Want To Be A Leader!* (Camp Hill, PA: Christian Publications, Inc. 1973), pp. 156–157.

4. Barclay, p. 74.

5. Sanders, pp. 140–141.

6. Engstrom, p. 121.

7. Jenson and Stevens, p. 121.

8. Gaines S. Dobbins, *Learning to Lead* (Nashville: Broadman Press 1968), p. 64.

Chapter 14

1. W. Robertson Nicoll, *The Expositor's Bible* (Grand Rapids, MI: Baker Book House 1982), Vol. II, p. 655.

2. Swindoll, p. 142.

3. H.A. Ironside, *Notes on the Book of Nehemiah* (Neptune, NJ: 1978), p. 91.

4. Barber, p. 126.

5. Campbell, p. 77.

6. Ironside, p. 93.

7. Seume, p. 88.

8. Campbell, p. 82.

9. Ironside, p. 100.

10. Swindoll, pp. 163–164.

11. C. F. Keil and F. Delitzsch, *Commentary on the Old Testament* (Grand Rapids, MI: William B. Eerdmans Publishing Co. 1980), Vol. III, Part III, p. 254.

Chapter 15

1. Campbell, p. 100.

2. Albert Barnes, et. al., *Barnes' Notes on the Old and New Testaments Vol. IV.* (Grand Rapids, MI: Baker Book House 1981), p. 477.

3. Fensham, p. 247.

4. Derek Kidner, *Ezra and Nehemiah* (Wheaton, IL: Tyndale House Publishers 1979), p. 119.

5. Barber, p. 150.

6. Campbell, p. 102.

7. Fred Fisher, *Commentary on 1 & 2 Corinthians* (Waco, TX: Word Publishing 1975), p. 202.

Chapter 16

1. Campbell, p. 104.

2. Alan Redpath, *Victorious Christian Service* (Westwood, NJ: Fleming H. Revell 1958), p. 172.

Chapter 17

1. Redpath, p. 188.

2. Campbell, p. 115.

3. Ironside, p. 124.